TALES OF THE
CITY OF GOD

TALES OF THE
CITY OF GOD

CARLOS G. VALLES, S.J.

A Campion Book

LOYOLA UNIVERSITY PRESS
CHICAGO

Loyola University Press
3441 North Ashland Avenue
Chicago, Illinois 60657

Cover and interior design by Nancy Gruenke

Library of Congress Cataloging-in-Publication Data

Valles, Carlos G. (Carlos Gonzales), 1925–
    Tales of the city of God / Carlos G. Valles.
        p. cm.
    ISBN 0-8294-0750-2 (pbk.)
    1. Spiritual life—Catholic Church. 2. Christian life—Anecdotes.
3. Christianity and other religions. 4. Catholic Church—Doctrines.
I. Title.
BX2350.2.V175 1993
242—dc20   93-8938
                                                  CIP

CONTENTS

PREFACE TO THE AMERICAN EDITION

Scholars and other interpreters of the human experience have begun to see that the deeper side of life—call it the faith side—can be reached intuitively and richly when examined via story and myth. This principle has been long accepted where the religious education of children is concerned. Presumably, the imaginative, affective, and appreciative powers of children are readily activated when stories are the medium. Today it is realized that adults, too, have the same outstanding resources—expecially at deeper levels where the life-search grows more complex. Thus, Christian myths—symbolic stories presenting the ideals, attitudes, and values of a believing people—are receiving renewed attention from spiritual writers. Alternatively, myths are the Scriptures with emphasis on the Gospels as portraits of Jesus as mythological hero. As such, they speak primarily to our hearts and feelings, yes, even to the hearts of grown-ups.

Father Anthony de Mello in his outstanding books *Sadhana* and *The Song of the Bird* and now Father Valles, a close friend of Father de Mello and author of *Tales of the City of God,* are drawing upon traditions of the East to enrich Western spirituality and reawaken the latter to its root inspirations. Judging by the reception to date, thousands of readers and hearers have been ready for this approach and have responded gratefully. As publisher of several of Father Valles's books, Loyola University Press is happy to make another example of this genre available.

Rev. Joseph F. Downey, S.J.
Editorial Director
Loyola University Press
May 1993

ONCE UPON
A TIME . . .

This book originated in a request my Spanish publisher, Jesús García-Abril, made me. "Carlos," he told me, "you must write a book of stories as Tony de Mello did. Write your own *Song of the Bird*, or whatever you want to call it. Do it at your own time and in your own way, but by all means do it. Think about it and let me know. I'll be waiting for it." I have a very deep respect for my publishers, not only because the very existence of my books depends on their good pleasure, but also because they usually have a fine sense of what readers want to read and writers can write and an intelligent hint on their part can mark the birth of a timely book. Besides, in this case, I knew from the start that the publisher was right.

I know the importance of the story, the beauty of an allegory, the innocence of a comparison, the smile of an anecdote, the spark of a joke, the depth of a parable. To say everything while saying nothing, to amuse without binding, to open windows without compelling to look through them, to have a good time and perhaps change a life. My own readings and my preparation of public talks and of books in several languages had already built up in my mind a thick file of experiences and episodes that could at short notice become the requested book. In fact I myself had thought of writing such a book, but I had been kept back by a nagging consideration. Though I believe my books to be quite independent and personal, circumstances had led me to work somewhat under Tony's shadow, and to write a book of stories for readers who have enjoyed *The Song of the Bird* and *The Prayer of the Frog* could appear to be imitation, competition, impudence, or just a mean trick to use another man's success to foster one's own. This is why I stalled.

Brahms did not publish his first symphony until twenty years after he had begun composing it, and the delay was caused by the shadow Beethoven's memory cast on the complicated, introverted, worked up, coiled up character that Brahms was. Who could dare to write a symphony after Beethoven's Ninth, which was the greatest masterpiece of all music of all times? Nothing was possible after the ultimate perfection of the supreme genius. Brahms came immediately after that, and he suffered from his place in history. He debated with himself, he hesitated, composed, suppressed, added, changed, improved, spoiled, filed, waited, and at long last published his expected and belabored symphony. And a fine work it was in its own right, with a very personal seal and typically different. Some such feeling, though by no means so tragic and overpowering, made me wait with my tales. But I'm not going to wait for twenty years, so here they are now.

I have enjoyed writing this book, perhaps more than any other I have written. It is much more amusing to tell a story than to compose a whole volume. I have felt lighter giving up the serious tone of the essay, ignoring the connection between chapters, forgetting the exacting plot of a single theme, the logic of the arguments, the link of the ideas, the thesis to be proved; and letting free my imagination, my sense of humor, my curiosity, the imp within me that is longing to jump into action with the mysterious gesture, the mischievous wink, the solemn voice, and the eternal charm of the magic words "Once upon a time . . . "

Carlos G. Valles, S.J.
St. Xavier's College
Ahmedabad, India
1992

ARE YOU READY?

This first story is, as indeed are all the others, a story I am telling to myself. I do not propose it as a teacher but as a student. I want to make clear to myself where the key of all learning lies—in the open mind, the eager inquiry, the innocent readiness to accept ideas and persons and situations and novelties with the generous hospitality of a truly universal heart, and in the courageous liberation from fears and cautions and routine and prejudice, letting the winds from any direction and of any origin play unhindered in the spaces of the soul. Wisdom is made up of curiosity, interest, adventure, and humor. The gates of wonder have to be kept open for all guests in the festival of life. Here is the little story.

A newly arrived inquirer
asked Sufi Jalaluddin Rumi:
"Master, are you ready to teach me?"
To which the master,
looking steadily into his eyes,
answered searchingly:
"Are you ready to learn?"

The question tears the soul apart with unforgiving brightness. Our first instinct is to protest in anger. Is it not enough to have come in search of the master, to wait for admittance, to think out the question, to express it, to beg for an answer? Is it not enough to take the book, to find the passage, to read intensely, to understand, to take note, to comment, to remember? Is it not enough to present a whole life of dedication, effort, study, and contemplation with its silence and darkness and daring and hope? Is not my whole being always, and my presence here today, saying abundantly that I want to learn and I claim it and this is what I have come for and what I ask with all the warmth of my soul in the urgency of my voice? Are you ready to teach me, master?

But then, am I ready to learn? Or am I led only by mere curiosity, superficial desire? Mere routine, mere repeating what others say, a show of knowledge, of saying, "Of course I know about it, I am in it, I have seen it, I have read it." And it is fine, no doubt, it is amusing and interesting, but I stay as I am, because I already knew everything before. Certainly, I will continue to search for a definitive light that may change my life and lift me to higher levels of spiritual achievement, but for the time being there is nothing to be done. Do I really mean that I will continue to search, or am I lying to myself? Do I search in earnest or only halfheartedly? Do I really go for it, or do I stop to bargain? Do I open my windows wide, or do I open them only a little so that I may say that the outside air comes in, though I sit in a stuffy room?

I have reason to question myself. Why is it, I ask myself, that sometimes a story does not stir me at all when I first read it, but when I read it again years later I suddenly feel shaken and overwhelmingly wrenched from the roots of my being, and the story haunts me and bewitches me and pitilessly imprints its unavoidable lesson in my mind? The story was the same, but I was not. When I first read the story I was closed to that new approach, and I saw nothing, whereas subsequently I had lowered my defenses, had removed the protective mask, had opened myself without reserve, and the arrow had flown straight and had hit the target. Why does a story impress one person and yet say nothing to another who seems very similar to the first? Why is it that the first time I read a certain author I discarded him after a few pages with lack of interest but that years later he became my favorite? I am not judging myself, let alone anyone else, but I have come to know a good deal about the reluctance, the defenses, the escapes, and the subterfuges that my subconscious brings into play in order to escape having to accept new ideas, adopt new attitudes, walk new paths. The master knows it, and that is why he makes this single and pointed question that is at once test and condition for accepting the candidate: Are you ready to learn?

Great has been my resistance against the light, and now I acknowledge it and want to expose myself to the kind brightness of stories and legends, of tales and parables, which say everything while saying nothing, which do not argue or discuss, do not convince or demonstrate but open up with a smile fields of sunlight for those who want to see and paths of truth for those who want to walk and, in any case, offer disinterestedly glimpses of wisdom to those who want to spend a happy and easy time loitering among the knowledge of centuries.

The whole world is a parable that is ready to teach me. Am I ready to learn?

THE HIDDEN STAR

The stars were celebrating their own assembly,
and each one was bringing to light,
as only stars can bring things to light,
its own merits in the life of humankind, crown of creation.
The polestar showed how it helped the people on earth
to fix north in their maps and in their journeys.
The sun described the warmth, the light, and the life
that it had engendered for all people on earth.
A little-known star revealed that it was the one
that had confirmed Einstein's theory when it passed
in the nick of time behind the sun during an eclipse
and with that had rendered a signal service to science.
And others mentioned the names they had made famous
and the discoveries they had given rise to.
Each one had something to say,
and they all rivaled in fame and splendor.

Only a little star, hidden and remote,
remained quiet in the celestial assembly.
It had nothing to say.
When its turn came and it had to say something,
it confessed that it had done nothing for the cosmos
or for the human race and that the people
on earth did not even know it,
as they had not yet discovered it.
The other stars laughed at it and reviled it
as useless, lazy, and unworthy to occupy a place in the sky.
The stars are there to brighten the heavens,
and what is the use of a star
of which not even the existence is known?

The little star was listening in silence
to all the reproaches its companions were hurling at it,
and then something occurred to it while the others spoke,

and it said it at the end.
"Who knows?" it said twinkling softly,
"maybe I, too, am contributing in my own way
to the progress and welfare of people in that far-off earth.
It is true that they do not know me, but they are no fools,
and their calculations tell them that,
in order to explain the paths
of other stars and heavenly bodies they know,
there must still be some other star whose gravitational
    attraction
will explain the observed deviations in their orbits.
This keeps them studying and observing and searching,
and that is the way their science advances
and their interest is kept awake."
The other stars had gradually fallen into silence
as the little star spoke, and so it gathered courage
and at the end said something that set all the other
    stars thinking:
"Not that I want to push myself forward in any way
or underestimate anybody else's work,
and indeed I am the first to recognize and proclaim
all the many good things you have done for the
    people on earth,
but I also think that I am rendering them
an important service: I am making them realize
that there is still something left for them to discover."

Beautiful message. There are still stars to discover. There are still heavens to explore and adventures to undertake and thoughts to risk and experiences to brave. Let no one think that the limit has been reached, that everything is known, that the map is perfect. On the spiritual map of our lives there is still an unknown land, a terra incognita as on medieval maps, full of dragons and monsters and sirens, which lends interest to our wanderings by leaving the world open. The greatest favor that can be done for us is to be made to realize that there are still stars to discover.

In my mathematics class at college a very intelligent but very naive student asked me one day: "How many theorems are there in geometry?" I laughed heartily in the middle of the class. That young man believed, and many with him, that geometry was a closed domain, a fixed science, a complete catalog and that its theorems could be counted like the days of the year or the trees in an orchard. So many and no more. That good lad wanted to find out how big a portion of geometry he had studied already and how much was left, and he was asking the question not with reference to the course for the examination but to geometry as such in its totality. "How many theorems are there in geometry?" We may count the number of theorems in Euclid's Elements, but geometry has traveled a good deal since then and will continue to travel without end through virgin lands with new results and unsuspected theorems. There are always stars left to discover. The beauty and challenge and charm of knowledge lies precisely in the fact that it has no end.

Stephen Hawking has said repeatedly that when we finally discover how the world began, that will be the end of physics, as there will be nothing more to discover. The physicist who discovers that will earn the last Nobel Prize in physics, and there will be no more prizes, he says, because there will be no more physics. The genius is wrong. Physics will never be over because the human intellect will not be over, and the intelligibility of matter will never be over. Cosmic surprises are waiting for us at every corner, and the capacity and the zest to continue the search is what gives vigor to our efforts and sense to our life. It would be a sad thing to turn over, in our life time, the last page of the book of knowledge.

In my spiritual life and religious experience I suffered the common triumphalistic stage when I thought I knew everything, and that did me harm. I was a faithful follower of the best religion in the world, well-trained member of a prestigious religious order, responsible student of all the sacred sciences, which were taught with authority and accepted with docility. I could define each dogma, measure the morality of each action, judge every conscience, interpret every scripture. I had an answer for every query, a solution for every problem. And I boasted of it. I felt entitled to it after studying for so many years in the best of places. I thought I had mastered all the theorems in geometry.

Then little by little echoes from the distant star began to reach my ears—contact with reality, life in India, other religions, atheistic friends, obvious limitations, new horizons. My own map, accurate and detailed though it was, did not cover those lands. There were still regions to be explored, heavens to be plotted, stars to be discovered. I count as a happy hour in my life that in which I realized that there was still much left for me to learn, to see, to feel, to enjoy. I became a student in the school of life again.

I am deeply indebted to the many stars that have appeared through the years in the skies of my life. But perhaps the one I owe most to is that little star, remote and hidden, joyful and mischievous, anonymous and beloved, which keeps on playing hide-and-seek with the lens of my telescope. And I keep searching.

THE FROG
IN THE WELL

A whole colony of frogs lived in a large deep well.
They led their life, kept their customs,
found their food, and croaked their throats away,
filling with movement and sound
the shadowed depths of the hospitable well.
Their own isolation from the outside world protected them,
and they lived in peace,
alert only to avoid the fall of the bucket
someone occasionally threw from the top
to draw water from the well.
As soon as they heard the pulley screech, they raised
   the alarm,
ducked under water or clung to the wall, and waited there
holding their breath until the bucket full of water
was hauled up again and the danger passed.

A young frog, after diving for cover in one such
   bucket alarm,
began to think that the bucket,
instead of a danger, could be an opportunity.
Up there on top he could see a bright opening,
as of a wide skylight, whose aspect changed
with the day and the night and on which shown
shadows and profiles and shapes and colors
that suggested there was something worth knowing
outside of the well. And, above all,
there was the feared and expected appearance
of the lovely face of the young maiden with two
   golden plaits,
who for a brief moment each day bent over the side
   of the well
to throw in the bucket and pull it back.
All that had to be explored.

The young frog spoke,
and all the others came down heavily on him.
That has never been done.
It will be the ruin of our race.
Heaven will punish us.
You will be lost forever.
We have been made to live here,
and here is where we can do well and be happy.
Outside the well there is only desolation and destruction.
Let no one dare to flout the laws of our ancestors.
How can a young frog pretend to know better than
     our ancestors!
The young frog waited patiently for the bucket to be
     lowered again.
He crouched on the right spot,
jumped onto the pail at the exact moment,
was lifted up, and rose with it
to the wonder and horror of the amphibian community.
The council of elders excommunicated the runaway frog
and forbade any talk about him.
The dignity of the well had to be upheld.
Months passed without anyone mentioning him
or anyone forgetting him, when one good day
a familiar croak was heard over the side of the well.
All the curious frogs gathered below, and they saw
silhouetted against the sky the remembered profile of the
     enterprising frog.
Another frog appeared then by his side,
and seven baby frogs gathered round them.
All below were looking without daring to say anything
when the frog spoke from the top:
"Up here there is a wonderful world waiting for us.
There is water that runs, not like the water down there,

and there are soft green blades that sprout from the ground,
and it is a joy to move among them,
and there are plenty of little beetles and tasty insects
    everywhere,
and one can eat different things every day.
And then there are many frogs of many types,
and they are very cultured and very fine,
and I have married one of them, and we are very happy
and have the seven children you see here with us.
There is plenty of space for all of you here,
because the fields are immense
and one never sees the end of them."
Down below the official authorities
threatened the frog that if he came down
he would be executed for high treason;
and he said that he did not intend to come down
and wished all of them a happy time,
and he went away with his companion
and the seven little frogs.

There was a great uproar in the depths of the well,
and some broad-minded frogs wanted
to have a debate on the proposal,
but the authorities croaked them down,
forbade any mention of the disturbing incident,
and life went back to normal
within the steep walls of the dark well.

The next morning, when the girl of the golden plaits
pulled up the bucket from the well,
she was astonished to see that it was full of frogs.

There is a compound word in Sanskrit to denote narrow-minded
people who are satisfied with hearing what they have always

heard and doing what they have always done, which is what everybody does and what, so it seems, has to be done in order to have a safe and quiet life. The word is *kup-manduk* ("frog in the well"), and it has passed from Sanskrit to the modern Indian languages intact. It is considered a rather derogatory term.

Even so, the world is full of wells, and the wells full of frogs. And girls with golden plaits still get startled from time to time when they go to draw water in the morning.

SPACE REPORT

The report submitted by the crew of the spaceship from the Via Aquaea at the end of their study of planet Earth, undertaken with a view to establish an intercultural contact if this were deemed possible and profitable:

We have carried out the reconnaissance mission
that was entrusted to us, and we have been able
to observe at close quarters without being detected,
thanks to our supersonic screen, the whole surface
    of planet Earth
and the changes that regularly take place on it,
changes that we believe are caused by its greater
    or lesser distance
from the central star of their system
from which they receive light and heat.
After many observations and repeated tests
we have arrived at the conclusion
that there is both vegetable and animal life on the planet,
with a great variety of living beings,
which we have proceeded to study in detail.
The dominant species seems to be the smooth-skinned
    bipeds
who live in colonies with a rigid organization.
The said beings live in solid anthills,
mostly of rectangular shape, with separate cells for
    each subgroup or,
in some cases, for each individual.
They come out of those cells, all approximately at the
    same time,
covered with strange trappings of different colors
    and shapes,
though they all obey a general pattern that changes
    with the seasons.

Then they get into small surface capsules, each
    with four wheels,
which advance by fits and starts in crowded lines
along carefully designed lanes, some in one direction
and some in the opposite one, in a very strange pattern
for which we have found no rational explanation.
These machines make much noise
and let out a great amount of fumes, which,
if our conjecture based on the frequency
and quantity of such emissions is right,
provide the necessary atmosphere for their breathing,
and that is why they renew it constantly.
The noises also seem to be some kind
of prevocal communication by means of which
each individual can keep up contact with the group
while it is within its own capsule.
After some time on the same day the process is inverted,
and the capsules go back to the anthills they started from.
Once in them, as far as we have been able to observe
through the holes they have,
they set themselves before a small screen,
which is not missing in any cell,
and on which shapes and colors appear at the command
    of a button.
This may well be the way they get their food,
and that would explain why they cannot do without it.

We have studied with special interest
the way they govern their colonies.
The election of the head in a colony is a long and
complicated process that is almost the same
in all places we have observed.
During a long period in each colony

the whole life of its inhabitants seems to turn around
this single event as though the future of the colony
    depended on it.
This activity is in sharp contrast with the fact that
as soon as there is a new head of the colony no one seems
    to care about it,
and there is a universal conviction among them that all
    heads are the same.
We do not know how to reconcile
such a recurring display of energy
with such a routine administration the rest of the time.
Another strange phenomenon we have observed
is that great multitudes of bipeds gather together
with studied regularity in large oval amphitheatres,
from whose rows of seats in multiple tiers they watch,
engrossed, a small number of their kind
performing quick and strange movements,
for which we have not been able to find a pattern,
propelling all the time a small spherical object of larger
    or smaller size.
They display very great excitement while the bizarre
    rite lasts.
We conjecture that this may have some connection
with the sexual cycle of the species,
but we have not been able to confirm our hypothesis.

The least understandable of all our observations
is the fact we have verified again and again,
in the midst of our own astonishment and grief,
that the bipeds often attack one another
without any reason or motive that may justify
    the aggression,
and this happens between individuals, groups,
and sometimes entire clans for long periods.

There is nothing in our own experience and
makeup that could explain such absurd behavior.

For all the above reasons we have arrived
at the final and clear conclusion that
the smooth-skinned bipeds are not rational beings,
that intelligence has not yet made its appearance
    on planet Earth,
that it will take still many cosmological ages to appear,
and that, in consequence, it would serve no purpose
and indeed would be meaningless to try to establish
    any kind
of cultural contact with the beings that today inhabit Earth.
Our mission is over.

After that come the signatures of all the scientists on board the
spaceship and the date of the report, which, when translated to
our own calendar, marks the year of the Christian Era in which we
happily and ignorantly live. They had a safe return journey to their
galaxy. A copy of their report fell accidentally on earth and is the
one reproduced here.

THE
UNBENDING
BRIDGE

Why does it rain when I go out dressed in a new suit? Why do I catch a cold when I most need to work? Why are there tornadoes and earthquakes? Why does death visit the persons we love most and at the moment we expect it least? Couldn't nature be a little more understanding, think of us who suffer the onslaught of its winds and its microbes, be a little more accommodating with us and spare us unnecessary crises? We do accept the general laws that are necessary for the smooth running of the universe, but couldn't our situation in each case also be taken into account so that we may avoid personal sufferings that achieve no purpose? Couldn't the rain wait a little, couldn't microbes be restrained, couldn't death be postponed? Couldn't mother nature be a little more of a mother?

Here is an experience and the consequent reflection on it of Rabindranath Tagore:

One day when I was sailing in the river
under a bridge, the mast of my boat
hit one of the arches of the bridge.
It would have been better for me
that the mast had bent a few inches,
or that the bridge should have arched its back like a cat,
or that the volume of water in the river
should have decreased a little.
But none of them did anything to avoid the collision.
And it is that quality precisely, that firmness
in each of the elements involved, that makes it possible
for me to sail on the river and hoist my mast
and count on the bridge to cross the river
when the current is not favorable.

This unbending rigor to be found
in the reality of things is bound to clash
with our wishes and lead us to grief,

just as the hardness of the
ground is unavoidably painful
for the child who falls while learning to walk.
And yet that same hardness that hurts him
is what makes it possible for the
child to walk on the ground.[1]

Laws are laws, and whims create chaos. The law hurts us when it clashes with our immediate interest, but it protects and shelters us in the open realm of our daily existence. We would be delighted to see our mast bend or the bridge heave to avoid the clash that is going to hurt us. But if masts bent and bridges heaved at will, we would never be able to sail seas and cross bridges. It is healthier to be hurt for once, and so to be reminded, however painfully, that creation has its norms and that our salvation lies in respecting and accepting them. We all have hurt our knees when we were small and stumbled and fell, and thanks to those scars of our childhood we can walk and run today along the paths of life, sure as we are that they will hold our step. Acceptance of the whole, even if the details at times mortify us—that is the way the universe works.

---

[1] Adapted from Rabindranath Tagore, *Sadhana* (Madrid: Editorial Afrodisio Aguado 1957), 100.

FIREWORKS

Rabindranath Tagore:

In the Ramayana, when Sita, forcibly abducted
from her husband's side, is bemoaning her sad fate
in Ravana's golden palace, she sees a messenger,
who approaches her and shows her the ring
of her beloved Rama. The sight of the ring
is enough to prove to Sita that the message is genuine.
She becomes immediately certain
that this messenger comes from her beloved
and that Rama has not forgotten her
and is getting ready to rescue her.

A flower is also a messenger
from our great lover.
In the midst of all the bewitching luxury of this world,
comparable to Ravana's golden city,
we live always in exile, while the insolent spirit
of material prosperity seduces us with its wiles,
seeking to possess us
as wicked Ravana wanted to possess Sita.
And in that prison, the flower comes to us,
bringing a message from the other shore,
and murmuring in our ear:
"I am here. It is He who sends me.
I am a messenger of Him whose
beauty equals only his love.
He has built a bridge to reach up to your loneliness.
He is coming to fetch you. He will take you to himself
and hold you in his arms.
Violence and deceit will not keep you
a prisoner forever."

If on that moment we are awake, we ask:
"How shall we know that it is He who sends you?"
The messenger answers:
"I bring His ring. See the splendor of its shining."
And in truth the ring is His ring, our own wedding ring.
We then forget everything.
This sweet symbol of eternal love
fills us with deep longing.
We realize that the golden palace in which we live
has nothing in common with us.
Our liberation is outside it,
where our love flowers and our life burns.[2]

When faith responds to love, the whole of creation becomes a temple that speaks of the presence of the Beloved. The ring. The flower. The wind. The sky. And, more cogently, every occasion and every circumstance and every work. Tagore draws from his own insight a practical and far-reaching conclusion. With such a vision, he says, "The furnaces in a factory become fireworks in a festival; the noise of machinery turns into a sweet melody." It is easy to see God in a flower. It is much more difficult to see him in a furnace or a machine. And yet, this is what true faith can do. To see God in the traffic of the city and in the work at the office, in routine and noise, in monotony and fatigue. That is the true art of living. Blessed be the worker who can see festive fireworks in the furnaces of the workshop and listen to melodies in the noise of its machines. Blessed are we when we see God in trial and suffering, in labor and toiling. When there is faith, everything has a message; when there is love, everything speaks. And the prison cell in the palace of the wicked king becomes a waiting room for the Beloved, whom we know to be near. Rama arrives in time and saves Sita. The Ramayana goes on.

---

[2] Adapted from Tagore, *Sadhana,* 140.

THE OTHER
SHORE

Rabindranath Tagore:

I shall never be able to forget a certain refrain
that I heard once at dawn
in the midst of the din of a crowd
that had gathered for the vigil on the eve of a great feast:
"Boatman, take me to the other shore!" said the refrain.
And I think that in the middle of the constant agitation
that our cares bring,
the call continues ever to be heard:
"Take me to the other shore!"

The bearer who in India pushes his cart along sings:
"Take me to the other shore!"
The vendor who peddles merchandise
from street to street sings:
"Take me to the other shore!"
And what is the meaning of this universal call?
It echoes, no doubt, the sensation we have
that we have not yet reached our goal.

But, is there anything more?
Where is the other shore? Is it something different
from what we already have?
Is it different from where we are now?
Not by any means. We are seeking our future destiny,
and it is in the very heart of our activity.
We are asking to be taken to a new place,
and this is the very place we are in now.

In truth, oh Ocean of bliss! this shore
and the other shore embrace in you a single shore.
When I say "this, my shore,"
the other becomes foreign to me,

and when I lose the sense
of the fullness that is in me,
my anxious heart claims "the other shore."
All that I have and all that seems alien to me
wait eagerly to be reconciled forever in your love.[3]

Our first desire to reach the other shore springs from within, from our heart, which knows itself to be far from its center and understands its mission to reach, beat by beat, the abode of peace and love. Soon we realize that it is not so much a question of "reaching" as of "being taken," as our oars are of no avail against the distance and the current and we need the friendly wind to blow and direct, push and persevere until we reach the other bank.

This inner desire that conquers all and rules all soon projects itself onto our surroundings. Then each voice, each sight, each figure, each circumstance in life sounds in our ears with the same longing. Then it is the bearer with his cart, the vendor with his goods, the child with his game, the bird with its trill, the tree with its leaves, and the sky with its stars that speak to us of the same yearning and that echo the universal prayer: Take me to the other shore! The whole universe vibrates with the single longing of a common goal.

And then comes the great awakening, the noble discovery, the exploding dawn that suddenly unveils a new revelation: the ocean in which we live has no shores. The notion of "this" shore or "the other" shore is illusory. It is not a question of reaching but of knowing that we have arrived. It is not a question of looking through the telescope but of opening our eyes. It is not a question of discovering shores but of enjoying the ocean. Peace, fullness, and bliss are right here. Here, now—taste of eternity on mortal lips, anticipated heirloom in present possession, promise

---

[3] Adapted from Tagore, *Sadhana,* 204.

that becomes reality, faith that blooms into experience, joyfully hidden seed that knows itself to be flower.

The smile keeps on singing, knowing that the song is as true as it is beautiful and knowing that now it can sing the song full voice because it knows the meaning of the song and transcends its melody in fervent dialog with the boatman who understands the human message that travels divine routes: Boatman, take me to the other shore!

BLUEPRINT
FOR A HOUSE

Mulla Nasrudin decided to have a new house
 built for himself.
He had a friend who was an architect,
and he went to see him to secure his services
in planning and building the new house.
The architect willingly accepted and asked him
for details about the type of home he wanted
so he could begin thinking about the plans.
"Tell me what kind of house you want,
how many rooms, bedrooms, bathrooms,
whether you want a garden or a lawn,
what your budget is, and, in fine,
whatever directions you,
and perhaps, even more, your wife,
can give me so that I can plan a house
that will be entirely to your liking."
The Mulla answered:
"Yes, my wife has given more thought to the matter
than I have, and she has told me to tell you this.
Look," he added, taking an old doorknob from his pocket,
"my wife is very much attached to this old doorknob,
and we want our house to match it.
That is all I can tell you."

The doorknob is the preconceived idea—a belief, a tradition, a prejudice, a custom. We carry it in our pocket, we keep it carefully, we take it out at the right moment, and we want everything else to fit in with it. Never mind how many rooms there are in the house, whether it is to face north or south, whether it will have three stories or only one. What matters is the doorknob. Let everything match it. That is all we want. We force meanings, change concepts, ignore advances in thought and life and behavior so that the doorknob can fit in. We are so fond of it that we have kept it until today and want to preserve it at all costs. The whole blueprint must be adapted to it. Never mind the results, the doorknob must be accommodated. Few things do more harm in life than a fixed idea, and we have many more than we imagine. We have only to search our pockets.

If I were the architect, I would have built their whole house in the shape of a doorknob! Maybe then they would open their eyes!

THE PRICE
OF A SMILE

"Mommy, why do you show such a lovely face on TV
and such a sour one at home?"
the small child asked her mother,
a famous television talk show host.
"Because when I am on TV they pay me for smiling,"
answered the TV star with spontaneous sincerity.
"And how much would you have to be paid
to smile at home?" asked the innocent child.
And the popular star felt her eyes go wet
as she embraced her child.

A television talk show host declared in an interview (in which she, for once, had to answer questions instead of asking them) that the hardest thing for her was to cope with the contrast between the image of herself she projected onto the screen and the real character she knew and had to live with day to day. "People know only my face on the screen with my smile and my glamour and my witty remarks that help them to enjoy my show, and they think I am always like that. But I am not. On the contrary, I have to unwind in my private life and let off steam to smooth down all the tensions brought about by my smiles and my wit during the two-hour program. And people around me refuse to accept me as I really am because they want me to be as I appear on the screen."

All of us, whether we work in television or not, have an image that we have projected through attitudes and conversation and reactions and preferences over the years. Our friends know that image and file it carefully in their minds and expect us to behave according to it because it is the one they know, and they demand that we, too, respect it and follow it. That is bondage. We are always obliged to smile as we smile on the screen, to say what we are expected to say, to behave as we have always behaved. This confinement makes change impossible and rules out all spontaneity. It makes home life difficult for the famous talk show host.

If the image is negative, if our friends and acquaintances have a poor opinion of us, it will be next to impossible, no matter how much we try to improve, to make them think well of us, or even to make them admit we have corrected some defects or smoothed out sharp edges. Before them we are always what we were in the old image, and any effort to change it will only succeed in emphasizing it for those who know it and enforce it on us. And, if the image is positive, if people hold us in esteem and appreciation, this also enslaves us in the long run, as it binds us to follow the pattern they have drawn for us under the rigid injuction that we continue to be what we have always been.

The "bad" boy is never trusted, and the "good" boy is never allowed any mischief. The image is slavery, under whatever sign it comes. This social imposition stifles the urge to experiment, the adventure, the risk, the attempt to find new patterns of behavior that will enrich our lives but that do not fit into the frame into which society has forced us and from which it does not want us to escape, as it would be inconvenient for society to have to adjust. Society freezes us with its demands of a repeated and expected routine, and then we, out of laziness, shame, fear, and indecision, find it hard to change our image and prefer to follow the easy furrow of the acquired custom. We are slaves to our own image, and our whole life is in chains for it. If we want to grow, we must break those chains.

The great liberation for humankind is the liberation from the image—the breaking of the mold, the slipping out of the frame, the departure from the stage. We must learn how to smile at home, without makeup, without floodlights, without rehearsal, and without pay. That is the most precious smile of our lives.

♪ ♪ ♪

THE TENOR'S
VOICE

Someone once asked the painter Dali:
"Is there any way, any sign or test
to recognize a genius?"
He answered forthwith:
"Of course there is. It is quite easy.
If he is born in Figueras, is a painter,
and is called Dali, he is a genius."
(Figueras was, of course, his own birthplace).

Apart from the wit and the self-assured confidence of this answer, there is something in it that is very true and very instructive. Geniuses do not need any visiting card or identity certificate but make themselves known by their very presence. They manifest their outstanding character in every gesture, every action, every word. Geniuses have no need to show credentials; they carry them in their own person. Their credentials are their very selves, and those who know this have no need to be told.

Of the tenor Caruso it is said
that once he had a problem in a bank
where he was asked to prove his identity
though he had no document with him
that could prove it.
So he opened his collar wide
and began to sing, full voice,
one of his favorite opera arias
in the middle of the bank . . .
and he cashed the check.

I sometimes quote these anecdotes when spiritual people, versed in the ways of intimate prayer, ask me about the experience of God. Was it real? How do I know it was he? How can I be sure? How can I distinguish it from the illusions and mere imaginings that can deceive us in such a delicate matter? The discernment of spirits has become an art, and its study is necessary for those who want to draw close to God. However, we must always always respect the inevitable veil our human condition holds in between. The basic and fundamental principle in this discernment is the recognition that God is his own proof. God brings his presence with him, and whoever has truly received his heavenly visit in his or her own soul does not need any proof or argument for it. The divine majesty carries its own glory; the Lord of the soul and of the whole of creation comes in and goes out without the need of a key and makes his presence felt without noise, and angels of peace form his retinue. "You are a Great Emperor in yourself," St. Theresa was wont to tell him, and that royal gait is the best guarantee of his immediate presence.

Indian mystics smile and say: "Those who have made love, know it." And what enamored religion has not likened the union of the soul and God to divine spousals? Prayer is a thing of love, and lovers know how to feel their mutual presence in the witness of their heart.

Let us by all means learn rules, study manuals, seek the advice of wise and holy persons, question ourselves, show prudence, and ask for light; but above all let us open our eyes, feel the presence, trust love itself, and learn to let God manifest himself in the depth of our souls with the royal sovereignty that is only his. Let the voice identify the singer.

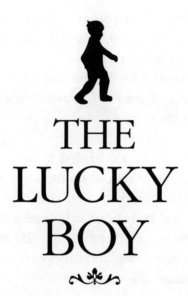

THE
LUCKY
BOY

A Brothers Grimm tale:

A boy had served his master for seven years,
and he asked for his earnings to take his leave
and return to his mother's house.
His master, pleased with his services,
gave him a piece of gold as big as his head
and let him go his way.

Gold is heavy, and the lad loaded it
on his shoulder as he set out on the long way home.
He met a man on horseback and began to think aloud
how nice it would be for him if he had a horse
instead of being weighed down with the gold.
The horseman heard him and proposed
that they exchange possessions.
The lad gave him the gold
and mounted happily on the horse.

After a while the horse reared up
and threw off the inexperienced rider.
As the lad was still on the ground,
a peasant came along with a cow.
The expected dialogue took place,
and the horse and the cow changed hands.

When the lad became thirsty
he tried to milk the cow,
but the animal gave him a kick
and left him senseless on the road.
In that situation he was found by a butcher
who was leading a pig to the slaughterhouse.
He explained to the boy

that the cow was too old to give milk
but the pig could give excellent sausages to last the
     whole year.
The deal was settled, and the lad took charge of the pig.

Not very far off he met a farmhand
who carried a goose, and who told him that,
in the village our lad was heading toward,
a pig had been stolen,
and he would come under suspicion
and have a rough time if seen there with his pig.
The lad was frightened and was filled with gratitude
when the obliging farmhand
allowed him to keep the goose in exchange for the pig.

The lad reached finally the last village
through which he had to pass on his way home,
and there he saw a knifegrinder
who sang happily as he sharpened knives.
The lad deduced that such a trade must bring happiness,
and readily gave his goose
for the two grinding stones the man offered him.

He went on his way, became thirsty,
and knelt down by a brook to drink,
but while bending down
the two stones fell out of his pocket
and were lost in the water.
The boy felt such a joy
when he saw himself rid of the last nuisance
in the long hike that he exclaimed
with spontaneous and genuine sincerity:
"I am the happiest man in the world!"

When he was young he dreamed he would change the whole world—society and politics and religion and culture. He would put an end to all injustice and all unbelief—a happy human race on a clean planet. The ideal was possible, and it was worth consecrating one's whole life to it. Any sacrifice was small, and difficulties would be only stepping stones to greater success. All people of goodwill would certainly rally round, and all together would carry out the noble deed. Humanity had suffered enough, and a new consciousness was now opening up sure paths of universal redemption.

As he became older his dreams became more modest. Maybe he could not liberate the whole world, but at least a good part of it. We have to admit that there will always be problems, because life is a struggle, but at least we shall be able to carry out a basic reformation that will prepare the way for a global campaign in its day. Never give up. If not in the whole world, at least in his own nation he would be able to effect a radical change, and that had to be accomplished by all means.

If not the whole country, at least his own social surroundings should be amenable to change, and that much had to be attempted and achieved as a help for some and an example for all. There was a circle his influence could certainly reach, and that had to be done for the good of all.

If society around him would not listen, at least his friends would do; and if not his friends, at least his own family would. One had to change mentalities, awaken consciences, reshape principles, improve behaviors. If we do not achieve that with the people with whom we share our daily lives, how can we succeed with the rest?

When even there he failed, after having struggled for it for the best part of his life, one day suddenly a light shone in his mind and he conceived a new and final resolution: The one to be reformed was . . . himself! That was the real goal. At last he had seen it. It was worthwhile to have slogged so much and to have changed the approach and to have advanced in life in order to see finally its true purpose: to improve ourselves. If he succeeded in reforming himself, he would have accomplished his mission in this world, he would have done all that he was expected to do, he would have set up an example, a center of reform, a sign and banner that would encourage others to do the same in their lives, and that would set in motion the only true revolution that could change the world. Reformation of his own self was the key and to that he pledged himself heart and soul, concentrating on the supreme and single task the multiple energies that had been dispersed along many battlefronts throughout his life. Now he knew his aim and would achieve his purpose.

And then one day, with all his life and all his experience behind him, with maturity of thought and clarity of vision, he sat down to rest and felt that the burden he had been carrying all along slipped gently away from him. He discovered, as through an angel's revelation, that there was no reason he should attempt to change himself, that it was useless for a start and impossible for an end, as his own sustained efforts had proved. The last two stones rolled away from the pockets of his soul, and they fell on the brook of life, lightening with their fall the burden he had carried through years of toil. He saw himself free, joyful, at peace with the world and with humankind and with God and with himself, and he shouted with all the strength of his now-youthful lungs for all creation to hear: "I am the happiest man in the world!"

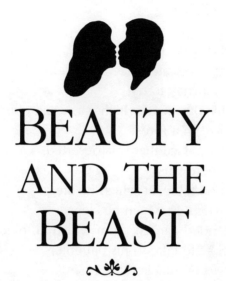

BEAUTY
AND THE
BEAST

This story is well known, so it will be enough to present a summary. The moral, however, is not so evident, and it may be worthwhile to comment on it.

A trader who had a daughter,
a true beauty in countenance as in name,
undertook a journey to try
to improve his business, which was at an ebb.
He became lost in a forest
and reached a palace that was deserted,
though in it there was
a well-provided table, at which he ate;
a furnished room, in which he slept;
and a well-tended garden, from which he plucked
a large red rose to take to his daughter.
No sooner had he plucked the rose
than a monster appeared and told him with a roar:
"I am the Beast, and all this belongs to me.
I did not mind that you ate at my table
and slept in my room, but I cannot forgive you
for plucking a rose from my garden.
Now you shall die."
The trader asked only for leave
to bid farewell to his daughter.
But she, on learning her father's plight,
offered herself to the Beast in place of her father,
and so it was done.

The Beast did Beauty no harm;
on the contrary, he treated her with kindness
and gave her every facility
that she might live in the palace at ease.
What is more, the monster one day proposed to her
and asked her to love him as he loved her.

She at first felt a great repugnance,
but she recognized that,
in spite of his gruesome appearance,
the Beast had a tender heart
and had behaved with great kindness toward her.
At length she accepted the proposal
and kissed the monster with tentative restraint.
At that very instant the Beast was transformed
into a handsome prince, who explained
how he had been under a spell
that could only be broken by a fair maiden's kiss.
The wedding and everyone's happiness soon followed.

The forests are full of princes who have been converted into animals and are waiting in their painful disguise for the kind care of a stray princess in order to become themselves again through the magic of love, which transforms all things. The Sleeping Beauty waits a hundred years in the castle, overgrown by brambles, for the valiant prince who will give her a kiss and awaken her. The very first tale told by the Brothers Grimm was "The Frog Prince," which teaches the same lesson.

A princess lost her golden ball in a well.
A frog offered to rescue it if the princess
promised to share her life with him.
The princess accepted.
She got back her golden ball
and pretended to forget the frog.
The frog followed her, and the king,
upon learning of the deal,
obliged his daughter to keep her promise.
The frog ate at her table and slept in her bed,
and, finally, a shy kiss unveiled the hidden prince.
Then the bells rang in a wedding once again.

The kiss frees the person. Love reveals the hidden beauty. When we feel we are appreciated, we begin to grow, to cheer up, to value ourselves, and to shine in all the beauty that is ours in body and soul. Many princes and princesses wander about in those enchanted forests, waiting for someone to kiss them that they may discover themselves, appreciate themselves, recover their confidence, their self-esteem, the courage to look in the mirror, to uncover their hidden beauty, and to come before the world without shyness and without fear, with the whole strength of their unique personality. The need is for people who know how to kiss—tenderly and gently, at the secret instant known to the stars alone—the expectant lips that need a kiss in order to flower into a royal smile.

Nothing helps us more to grow and develop in full our own personalities and characters than to know that we are appreciated, esteemed, and loved. Inside me there is a person who wants to be loved, independently from his successes or failures, who does not want to depend on appearances or circumstances, on youth or old age, on strength or weakness, on beauty or homeliness to take the place he desires in the hearts of those who surround him. There is a person who wants to be valued and loved as a person in the intimacy of his being and the uniqueness of his presence, who is waiting for unconditional and free and sincere love so that he may open himself to friendship and glory with all the richness that is inside him, and who will remain hidden until the kiss comes and the veil falls.

And, as I am waiting for the kiss to wake me up, I am also learning how to find and recognize the beauty that is in others under rustic disguises, and to bring to light, with my respect and my love, the latent gifts of those who, despite appearances, are worth so much. With a word, a gesture, a smile, a kiss, the spell of many years is broken. A face lights up, and a life is recovered. Once again the fairy tale finds its happy ending.

THE CAT
AS A MEANS OF
COMMUNICATION

A Hungarian tale:

A young man fell in love with a young girl
and asked her to marry him.
She agreed, with three conditions:
the husband would do all the housework,
he would never speak to her about it,
and he would never beat her.
The man agreed, and they married
and began their happy life together.

The husband began zestfully to do all the housework daily,
because he truly loved his wife and he had given his word.
But soon he became tired of having to do
all the work at home after his own work outside
while his wife amused herself all day
running around, singing, playing, and visiting people,
as she had nothing to do in the house or outside.
But the husband had pledged his word
and could tell her nothing, by word or by deed,
and so was forced to go on with his toil
day after day without help.

One day the man, before leaving for his work in the fields,
addressed himself to the cat that purred contentedly,
cuddled up in his favorite corner, and told him:
"Listen to me, you lazy and useless cat!
You spend the whole day there doing nothing,
while I must sweat in the fields the whole day,
and when I come home in the evening
I must clean the house and cook supper
and serve it and wash the dishes.
Now, this is over! When I come back this evening

I want the whole house to have been fully swept
    and cleaned
and supper cooked and served.
And woe to you if you don't do it!"
The cat remained undisturbed in his corner,
and the wife, who had heard everything,
took no notice of it and went as usual to run about
    the neighborhood
telling tales and listening to them.
The husband came back, saw the house dirty and the
    supper uncooked,
and making straight for the cat began to rebuke him,
to scold him sharply for not having carried out
    his orders,
and taking a stick he began to thrash him for not having
    done his duty.
The cat jumped to seek refuge in the woman's arms,
and the husband continued wielding the rod
without minding very much where blows fell,
all the time shouting at the cat and assuring him that
    the next day
it would go worse for him if the house and the supper
were not ready when he came home.

The same scene took place three days in succession,
and on the third day the woman, who,
what with the cat's scratching and the indirect blows
    of the stick,
had received a good beating,
decided to get the message and act accordingly.
She took up broom and duster, swept and scrubbed
    the floor,
lit the fire, and prepared a tasty supper,

which she ate peacefully and joyfully together with
her husband.
The cat, too, who had not quite understood the
strange proceedings,
got an extra ration to make up for the inconveniences
caused to him.

If the cat were able to speak, he would say simply: Why doesn't
he tell her straight all that he is telling me without my understanding a word? If many friends of many couples could speak when
the husband or the wife confide to them their difficulties in their
married life, they also would say clearly and directly: Why doesn't
he or she tell her or him all that he or she is telling me to no useful purpose?

Misunderstandings, in family life as well as among friends and in
society at large, come from lack of communication. People do not
speak; they do not tell each other what they ought to tell. They do
not let each other know what they think, what they feel, what
they resent in the other person, and this lack of information in the
things that matter creates a gap, a distance, an isolation, however
close they may live to each other. When people imagine what
their spouses are thinking they are usually mistaken, the miscon-
struing creates further estrangement, and they end up acting as
strangers to each other in spite of living in the same house.

The nonspeaking sickness may come simply from shyness, from
passivity, from fear to hurt or to be hurt, or from not having begun
on time and regretting now that it is too late to start. The result is
always the same. The couple does not talk. They do not talk
among themselves about the things they should talk about, and
without talking there is no understanding.

A cat is needed—a mediator, an instrument, an excuse. We
need a way to get our message across, to let the other person
know what we really think, what we need, what the other person
should know in order to adjust his or her behavior to the reality of

the two of us. We must break silence. We must learn how to speak. We are in the communication age, and communication has to begin at home. Telephone and radio and telex and fax are of no avail if they only help us to communicate with the whole world while they isolate us from our family. It is easy to invent machines for communication at a large distance. What is difficult is communication at close quarters.

The best marriage vow between husband and wife, the best pledge of loyalty between friend and friend is the firm and mutual determination to tell each other always, with tact and sensitivity, whatever one feels, desires, and expects with respect to the other. Whether something is done about these feelings later on is another matter, and the fact that things are felt does not mean that they are to be acted upon. What is essential is the external expression of the internal tension. If you are not convinced, you can ask the cat about it.

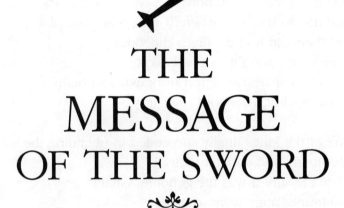

THE
MESSAGE
OF THE SWORD

In the time of war and strife between Moorish kings,
a legend spread from mouth to mouth that
whoever took possession of the sword Asharaf
would win the contest and would rule over all the
    lands of Islam.
Obtaining the sword, however, was no easy task.
One had to discover where it was, reach the place,
and then win it in deadly competition,
as everyone sought its possession.
The kings spared no effort of brawn and brain
to get hold of the sword of victory.

One of the kings finally succeeded in obtaining the sword
after many and difficult trials.
He made sure it was the genuine Asharaf,
and immediately went to battle,
wielding it against all the other kings.
He knew himself invincible
and was impatient to avail himself
of the power the sword conferred on him.
Yet things did not turn out quite as he had expected.
In his very first battle with the sword,
he was defeated and killed,
pierced through by the same sword
he was sure would bring him victory.
He died with his lips contorted in a painful grimace
that seemed to ask in surprise
how he could have been defeated.
If this were the genuine sword Asharaf,
how could it have let him down at the very first encounter?

The same surprise could be read on the faces of the victors,
who carefully pulled out the blood-stained sword
and examined it in detail.

The riddle then solved itself before their eyes.
Once cleaned of all the blood,
the sword revealed on its shining blade
a vertical inscription carved into it with artistic filigree
and written in intertwined Arabic characters for everyone
    to read:
"Never fight with the sword.
Through concord and understanding
will your brothers join you."
That was the message of the redeeming sword.
Its new master understood it, gave up violence,
    and sought peace,
and all the other kingdoms joined with him in
    fraternal unity.

Life is full of messages. Objects speak; events have meaning; circumstances reveal secrets that lead to victory. But we are in a hurry and do not stop to listen, to read, to decipher the code. We hear about a sword and assume that a sword is meant only to be wielded in battle, and there we go to fight madly, doing exactly the opposite of what the sword itself was teaching us in its artistically wrought blade. We rush into things. We itch for action, violence, confrontation. We have heard the legend, and our imagination runs wild. They all speak about it; we must follow the lead; we must get hold of the sword before our opponent gets it, and we must raise it before we have had time to discover its secret.

Wait a moment. Reflect. Have a good look at the sword in your hand. The sword is any activity, any plan for action, any ideology, any campaign, any slogan. Look at it well before you plunge. Read the message engraved on its shining blade. Find out for yourself. Do not rely upon outward appearances. It is possible that the sword is not meant to fight battles but to avoid them. Learn how to read. Get used to interpreting the messages that reach you through persons and events. Let circumstances speak. Open your senses wide before the signs of the times. Listen. Think. Let history whisper the wisdom of centuries in your ear. Develop eyes to see and ears to hear and sensitivity to feel. The whole of life is sacred hieroglyphics, artistic and secret, which must be deciphered step by step, stroke by stroke, moment by moment. The message, if understood in time, can save a kingdom.

Asharaf means "noble" in Arabic.

FOR GOD
AND
COUNTRY

This is a story Tony de Mello often told and never printed, and it may be worthwhile to rescue it from oblivion. For him, patriotism was not a virtue or anything meritorious in any way, but a mere conditioning imposed from outside and manipulated by others for selfish aims and with disastrous results as witnessed by history in all times and newspapers on any day. The division of land into states and nations is a practical need to cut down to manageable size the government of peoples, but such divisions are arbitrary in their boundaries and often violent in their origin. Frontiers cause wars, and those frontiers that are held sacred today were one day imposed by a foreign power through an unjust treaty. We have only to see the boundaries on the map of Africa, which seem to have been drawn by a straight ruler without any consideration of territories and races and tribes, or to look at the dividing line between India and Pakistan, which was drawn when the two countries became independent from Great Britain and separated from each other. Any such example is enough to see how absurd each state frontier is and how questionable the consequent concept of motherland is, however sublime and sacred it may be made to appear.

The wars between India and Pakistan are precisely the background of this story, though any border war in any century and between any countries could as easily be. Although Tony speaks about his own country ("Mother India" it is often called, and she is venerated and defended as such by her children in their teeming millions), he does so without prejudice to any other country, as his intention was to obliterate national differences by minimizing the importance and sacredness of the concept of country. His idea, however, was novel and daring and could lend itself to misunderstandings and opposition. Maybe that is why he never entrusted it to print. Whether the story was Tony's original or not I do not know for certain, but it bears his imprint on every line.

During one of the recent wars
between India and Pakistan,
some officers of the Pakistani army
were made prisoners by the Indians
and were kept under guard,
with all consideration due their rank,
until the end of the hostilities.
When the day came for them to be
returned to their country,
an Indian officer went to them, set them free,
accompanied them to the border between the
    two countries,
and told them: "That line of trees you see over there
marks the frontier between India and Pakistan.
Once you cross it, you'll be in your own land.
Good luck!"

The Pakistani officers were overjoyed
when they caught the first glimpse of their land.
They started running with all possible speed,
passed the line of trees,
and, once they were on Pakistani ground,
knelt down and began to kiss the earth,
shed tears of joy,
and say again and again:
"O Mother Pakistan!
We love you, we serve you, we venerate you!
We have suffered for you,
and we would be ready and honored
to suffer much more
and to give up our last drop of blood
to ensure your safety and perpetuate your glory.
To step on your sacred soil fills us with joy, O Mother!"

While the devout officers were thus
worshiping their motherland's soil,
the Indian officer came from behind,
running too and waving some papers in his hand.
When he reached the spot and succeeded in getting
the Pakistani officers' attention,
he told them: "Please, forgive me, sirs, if I interrupt you,
but it seems there has been a mistake.
I have just checked the map,
and Pakistan does not start along this line of trees,
but along the next one you see a hundred yards away.
The land on which you are now is still India.
Be kind enough to shift yourselves a little farther,
and you will be at home.
I hope I have not caused you any inconvenience
and offer you again my apologies."

When Tony told this story there was a long silence until someone
in the group asked: "Tony, with this you have demythologized the
concept of motherland. Would you do the same with the concept
of family?" Then Tony, who seemed to have been waiting for the
question, answered with another story.

A man who had just become a father
for the first time was taken by the nurse in charge
to the long, sterilized hall in the maternity ward
where the babies born that day were exhibited
in their parallel and identical cradles
in a monotonous show.
The nurse pointed to cradle number four
and left the man alone for his first encounter with his
     first child.
The apprentice father began looking at his child
with all the tenderness he was capable of

and began to try to attract the baby's attention—
to make gestures, to smile—
until it seemed to him that the child was smiling back.
He then began to feel within himself
the birth of the deepest and tenderest of feelings
that can grow in a man.
He was thus enraptured
when the nurse approached him gingerly
with some papers in her hand,
called him by name,
and, when she succeeded in getting
his attention, told him:
"Kindly excuse me for interrupting you,
but you are Mr. _____ aren't you?
You see, there has been a small mistake.
I have just checked the papers you see here,
and your son is not the one in cradle number four,
but the one in number six,
that is, two cradles to the right.
Yes, yes, that one is definitely your child
with absolute certainty.
You may examine the files yourself if you so desire.
I hope I have not caused any inconvenience,
and I ask you to accept my apologies."

No one dared ask Tony any more questions that day.

LEARNING
HOW TO
FLY

The resistance we can bring to bear against a new idea, a change, anything that may imply novelty, adventure, and risk is so instinctive and instantaneous that we can ourselves miss it, that is, we can resist without realizing we are resisting and can reject something before we consciously realize we have rejected it. This quick, hidden, and efficient resistance is the greatest practical obstacle we meet in the way of our personal growth. And the first step to remove this obstacle is to recognize its existence, to sense this resistance, to bring it to light and look it in the face in order to decide in freedom and responsibility what we want to do with it. We may heed its warnings and retrace our steps, or we may put it aside and go ahead along the new way. The decision could be any one at all; what is important is that we free ourselves from that blind resistance. We must learn to unmask it.

The theory is clear enough, but it is not much use by itself. I am going to give an example, as an anecdote can often prove more than an argument and a simple but true story can help more than a syllogism. When I deal with these topics before audiences, I foster a dialog with my listeners so that real communication takes place, so there is two-way traffic, and I learn from them as much or more than they from me. One of the things that I keep on learning, and never quite learn enough, is precisely the stalling force of this stubborn resistance that freezes the brain, dampens enthusiasm, and quashes adventure. Following is the story of a real and extreme case, which, after annoying me somewhat at first, made me laugh.

Once, when giving a public talk, I told the following story.

It was during one of those
eloquent attacks on the Self,
when nothing seemed to be left to do or not to do
in the dark night of the soul,
while Tony was ruthlessly hammering on this central truth,
closing every escape and invalidating every excuse,

and urging us on to total generosity
in spite of the difficulties of the task
that seemed to leave us suspended without support
between heaven and earth,
that I heard what was perhaps the most beautiful
and meaningful sentence I ever heard from Tony's lips.
He said: "When people hear me speak in this way
   they tell me,
'Tony, listening to you one is left with nothing
   to hang on to . . . '
and I then complete their sentence, adding
   in the same tone,
' . . . as the bird said when it began to fly.'
Now you know."[4]

After I told this story we were commenting on it in a group, all standing at the door of the hall and all free to take part in the discussion. There was keen interest to delve into the dark meaning of that total surrender, that night of faith, that jump into the void that, to be effective, must be as radical as the bird's first seemingly suicidal flight from the sheltering nest to the abyss. All had understood perfectly well the beautiful comparison, meant to illustrate the common doctrine of all great spiritual masters of all times that we must give up all in order to gain all. "When you stop at something," St. John of the Cross said in an expression that best describes the bird in the story giving up every support to achieve flight, "you miss the Whole."

That was what we were discussing when a middle-aged nun approached the group and, from its edge, interrupted our conversation, and shaking her finger at me she said quickly and dictatorially: "But the bird had the air on which to lean, it had the air . . . "

---

[4] You may find this story in my book on Tony de Mello, *Unencumbered by Baggage* (Anand, India: Gujarat Sahitya Prakash), 98.

And before anyone could answer her, she turned and disappeared in a hurry.

Quite a smart woman. She had found the way to pull to pieces all that had been exposed in the morning. She successfully withstood the idea of total renunciation, not of material goods but of ideas, customs, traditions, and practices that protected her life and regulated her behavior. She had inwardly rebelled against the call to total detachment, and since she was not lacking in intelligence, she looked for the crack in the argument, and she found it. The bird's surrender was not total, because he had the air. She said it and ran away. She must not have been very sure of her ground. Or of her air.

Every comparison stands on what was called in Latin the *tertium comparationis* (that is, the point of contact between the idea and the image), and, when exploring comparisons, one ignores all the details that are necessary for the picture but are not relevant for the comparison. Otherwise, we would have to say that the bird has wings though human beings have none and so the comparison is not valid, but all know that this negation is not valid. All, that is, except those who do not want to know it. And they do not want to know it because they are afraid of knowing it. They then find the witty answer, the easy escape, and avoid the pain of having to face themselves. That is, they miss the occasion to look at themselves, to know themselves, to grow. The escapist is always the loser.

The escape usually takes place through the intellect. We are very clever. A bit of logic, a fallacy, a contradiction, and the most beautiful comparison can be wrecked. Reason cheats us. On the contrary, when our whole sense, our instinct, our heart, our living organism leads us gently on to something, that is the right choice. But reason wants to rule over all; it finds a subtlety and vetoes the advance—sad history of a thousand failures to grow.

The good sister went away with the smile of victory on her lips, yet it was she who had hurt herself. If her attitude helps us to recognize and understand the defenses we instinctively put up before every new challenge, her example will have helped us to lower defenses and advance in life. Who knows? Perhaps she herself in the safety of her own privacy has tried her wings and has learned how to fly, with air or without it. I would feel happy if she had.

GOOD LUCK?
BAD LUCK?

Tony de Mello's readers know the importance he gave to the story "Good Luck? Bad Luck?" which teaches that we never really know whether a concrete event is going to be good or evil for us in the long run, an attitude that helps to bring a balanced perspective to our vision of things and helps us to acquire patience in adversity and moderation in success. He used the Chinese version of the story, and in my book about him I have given the Indian version. Here I present the Sufi version, attributed to Sheikh Mohamed Jamaludin of Adrianople, who died in 1750, as is found in Idries Shah's collection *Tales of the Dervishes.* The editor mentions there that the story is also well known in Greek folklore. The important lesson it teaches seems, therefore, to be part of the universal conscience of humankind.

Once in a city in the Farthest West
there lived a girl named Fatima.
She was the daughter of a prosperous spinner.
One day her father said to her:
"Come, daughter; we are going on a journey,
for I have business in the islands of the Middle Sea.
Perhaps you may find some handsome youth
in a good situation whom you could take as husband."

They set off and traveled from island to island,
the father doing his trading
while Fatima dreamed of the husband
who might soon be hers.
While they were on the way to Crete, however,
a storm blew up, and the ship was wrecked.
Fatima, only half-conscious,
was cast upon the seashore near Alexandria.
Her father was dead, and she was utterly destitute.

She could only dimly remember her life before then
because her experience of the shipwreck
and her exposure in the sea had utterly exhausted her.

While she was wandering on the sands,
a family of clothmakers found her.
Although they were poor,
they took her into their humble home and taught her
    their craft.
Thus it was that she made a second life for herself,
and within a year or two she was happy and reconciled
    to her lot.
But one day, when she was on the seashore for
    some reason,
a band of slave-traders landed and carried her,
along with other captives, away with them.

Although she bitterly lamented her lot,
Fatima found no sympathy from the slavers,
who took her to Istanbul and sold her as a slave.

Her world had collapsed for the second time.
Now it chanced that there were few buyers at the market.
One of them was a man who was looking for slaves
to work in his woodyard, where he made masts for ships.
When he saw the dejection of the unfortunate Fatima,
he decided to buy her, thinking that in this way, at least,
he might be able to give her a slightly better life
than if she were bought by someone else.

He took Fatima to his home,
intending to make her a serving-maid for his wife.

When he arrived at the house, however,
he found that he had lost all his money
in a cargo that had been captured by pirates.
He could not afford workers, so he, Fatima, and his wife
were left alone to work at the heavy labor of making masts.

Fatima, grateful to her employer for rescuing her,
worked so hard and so well that he gave her her freedom,
and she became his trusted helper.
Thus it was that she became comparatively happy in her
    third career.

One day he said to her: "Fatima, I want you to go
with a cargo of ships' masts to Java, as my agent,
and be sure that you sell them at a profit."

She set off, but when the ship was off the coast of China
a typhoon wrecked it, and Fatima found herself again
cast upon the seashore of a strange land.
Once again she wept bitterly, for she felt that nothing
    in her life
was working in accordance with expectation.
Whenever things seemed to be going well
something came and destroyed all her hopes.

"Why is it," she cried out, for the third time,
"that whenever I try to do something it comes to grief?
Why should so many unfortunate things happen to me?"
But there was no answer.
So she picked herself up from the sand and started
    to walk inland.

Now it so happened that no one in China
had heard of Fatima or knew anything about her troubles.

But there was a legend that a certain stranger,
a woman, would one day arrive there
and that she would be able to make a tent for the Emperor.
And, since there was as yet no one in China who could
    make tents,
everyone looked upon the fulfilment of this prediction
with the liveliest anticipation.

In order to make sure that this stranger
would not be missed when she arrived,
successive Emperors of China had followed the custom
of sending heralds, once a year, to all the towns
and villages of the land,
asking for any foreign woman to be produced at Court.

When Fatima stumbled into a town
by the Chinese seashore, it was one such occasion.
The people spoke to her through an interpreter
and explained that she would have to go to see
    the Emperor.

"Lady," said the Emperor
when Fatima was brought before him,
"can you make a tent?"

"I think so," said Fatima.

She asked for rope, but there was none to be had.
So, remembering her time as a spinner,
she collected flax and made ropes.
Then she asked for a stout cloth,
but the Chinese had none of the kind that she needed.
So, drawing on her experience with the weavers of
    Alexandria,

she made some stout tentcloth.
Then she found that she needed tent poles,
but there were none in China.
So Fatima, remembering how she had been trained
by the wood-fashioner of Istanbul,
cunningly made stout tent poles.
When these were ready, she racked her brains
for the memory of all the tents she had seen in her travels,
and lo, a tent was made.

When this wonder was revealed to the Emperor of China,
he offered Fatima the fulfillment of any wish she cared
    to name.
She chose to settle in China,
where she married a handsome prince
and where she remained in happiness,
surrounded by her children, until the end of her days.

It was through these adventures that Fatima realized
that what had appeared to be an unpleasant experience
    at the time
turned out to be an essential part
of the making of her ultimate happiness.[5]

I am going to add my own limited, though recent, experience to
the records of Sufi, Greek, Indian, and Chinese wisdom. While
writing this book, shortly before reaching this episode, my typewriter stopped working. That meant trouble for me. These elec-
tronic gadgets are a marvel while they work properly, but when
they go on strike they are a nightmare. I would have to send it for
repairs, and God knows how long the repairs would take and how

---

[5] Adapted from Idries Shah, *Tales of the Dervishes* (New York: E. P. Dutton,
1970), 72–74.

good they would be. I am mistrustful of machines. I trust people much more than I trust machines. Machines have let me down at the last minute and without previous notice as no person has ever done, and once a machine betrays me in such a way, as this had done now, I never trust it again. It may fail me again at any moment, and so I no longer feel at ease with it. Such was the case now. And the annoyance was even greater because I had become attached to it, and the breakdown looked like a betrayal to me. I was in a fix. Sheer bad luck. Or was it good luck? Who could tell?

I commented on the mishap to a friend, little suspecting how fast and efficiently he was going to react. The very next day he came to my place with a gift in his hand: the latest model of my own hospitalized instrument. I tried it on the spot. It printed better, used correcting ribbon, had automatic indentation and right-margin justification, paper feeding, half-space key, and decimal tabulator, all features that my previous model did not have. It was love at first sight, and with shameful fickleness and ungratefulness I did not even bother to send the old typewriter for repairs. Bad luck had swiftly turned to good luck.

And now I am eagerly waiting for this typewriter also to break down!

ROYAL WEDDING

The king told his daughter, the princess:
"I have arranged your wedding.
Your husband will be a young, handsome,
   and courageous prince,
who no doubt will bring happiness to you and honor
   to our kingdom.
The wedding will take place in fifteen days.
During these days you may enjoy yourself
as the innocent child you have always been
and thus take leave of a happy stage in your life
and enter the next one, which I hope will be even
   happier."
The princess felt great joy at the news,
told at once her companions and playmates about it,
and got ready to spend fifteen days in joyful freedom
before facing her new responsibility.

During the merry and carefree games and encounters
   of those fifteen days,
she came to know a young and cheerful young man,
and the blind destiny that rules the hearts of men and
   women
without regard to propriety or circumstances,
disposed that she should fall in love with him,
   and he with her.
Those few days of youthful carelessness
were enough to unite them in deep and exclusive love
before they realized what an impossible situation
they had plunged themselves into.
The eve of the royal wedding came,
and the princess opened her heart to her lover and
   revealed her plight:
"I am the king's daughter, and he has promised me
   in marriage

to a prince whom I am to wed tomorrow. I should
   have told you before,
but my love was faster than my words, and now
   it is too late.
I know what you suffer, and you know how I suffer
   and will suffer,
because my love for you is as strong as your love for me;
but know and remember that I will always be yours
   in my heart
until the end of my days and for all eternity.
And if God, who loves all lovers, hears me,
he will find a way to return me to you, and I will wait
   for you always."
The young man answered: "Your pain soothes mine,
because I, too, must marry whom my father has chosen
   for me;
but I, too, will be yours so long as I live, and yours shall
   I die."
The next day the wedding took place with full splendor.
The bride asked to be allowed to keep her veil down until
   the last moment,
a gesture that was interpreted as modesty,
though the truth was that she did so to hide her tears.
Finally the moment came to stand face to face
before the man who already was her husband.
She lifted her veil holding back her tears,
and he lifted the visor of his helmet.
The princess's tears dried up instantly at their source,
as she saw that the prince she had married
was none other than the young man with whom she had
   fallen in love.
He was the prince chosen by her father to marry her,
though neither of them knew it.
Their parents had arranged their marriage

without informing them about their mutual partners,
they had met by chance, had fallen in love without help,
and had found in the wedding the happy ending that,
for each of them, his or her partner was his or her love.
That was a truly happy wedding, and the parents,
when they saw how happy their children were,
congratulated themselves on the wisdom of their choice.

We do enjoy things to some extent on this earth—we love, we
play, we laugh, we talk, we eat, we travel, we amuse ourselves,
and we even reach some true and genuine pleasures at times—but
always with a hidden misgiving, with a little fear, with something
of a guilt complex. We have been taught that there is something
wrong with enjoying ourselves, that true pleasure and happiness
is something that belongs to the next life, not to this one, that the
one we must love is God, that we must seek him alone. Thus we
always feel a little remorse when we love someone deeply in this
world and we enjoy ourselves and have a good time. We are sup-
posed to marry the partner our parents choose for us.

I think that when the wedding comes and we go to heaven and
lift the visor and remove the veil, we are going to find that the
face we see reflects (with infinite beauty and serene majesty, to be
sure, but with uncanny fidelity and detail) the faces of all those
people we have loved in this life, that his smile echoes the joys we
have felt here, that his eyes mirror the landscapes we have
admired, and that his voice resounds with the songs we have sung
here on earth. The young man with whom we had fallen in love
was, without our knowing it, our betrothed. The pleasures of this
life were practice for heaven. Our neighbor—and in him or her
our companion, our friend, our lover—was God.

Let all the bells ring, for there is a royal wedding today.

A TON
OF RICE

A woman, who wanted to find peace
in the midst of her household chores as wife and mother,
came to the sage Yang Zhu and requested to be instructed
as fast as possible so that she could obtain illumination
    at once
and go back to her home with a quietened mind,
    convinced as she was
that, once her mind was liberated from the illusion
    that is life,
she could devote herself fully to her duties
without being troubled in the least.
She was therefore very keen on obtaining liberation
in the little time at her disposal
and was ready to do anything to achieve her purpose.

The sage answered: "Your desire is genuine,
and this is the first great condition to obtain the fruit
    of the spirit.
But some instructions and some practices are also needed,
and I can teach you little by little
in the short times you may have to come to see me.
After a great desire, the next requisite for illumination
is a great patience. You have told me you have a son.
In all his life your son will have eaten a ton of rice.
But what would happen if you made him eat all that
    rice at one time?
It would do him not good but harm.
Learn how to experience a great desire and no hurry.
Come back when you so desire."

Do not read this book too fast. Do not get indigestion.

THE
NOBEL
PRIZE

I can almost say that I have written this book in order to be able to tell this story. It occurred to me when I was trying to explain to audience after audience the reluctance we all feel when there is a question of giving up customs, attitudes, or beliefs that have lost their value but that we continue to treasure and cling to because we feel more comfortable in the old routine, are lazy enough to avoid having to try anything new, need to adjust to the way of thinking and acting of the group we belong to in order to feel accepted, and are afraid of the punishment that will ensue if we abandon tradition and embrace novelties. This reluctance, I believe and defend, must be brought to light, must be looked in the face, must be confronted squarely in order to decide later in clear conscience and explicit determination whether we want to carry on with our practice, whatever the reasons for or against it, or whether we choose, rather, to change our attitude and face the consequences. In this context the story is plain and simple, uncovers shyness, and encourages newness to be able to see old sights with new eyes.

But I soon realized that the story is dangerous. T. S. Kuhn has said that human beings have an infinite capacity to stick to their points of view against all evidence, and just by dealing a little with people who hold different points of view anyone can readily verify how true that statement is. Whatever a person has believed through the years becomes fixed, permanent, unshakable, and is defended against all evidence—all the more strongly as the evidence against it becomes greater. When anyone feels threatened, he or she brings into play all resources and skills in dialectics, pugnacity, and skulduggery and defends the cause as life itself. So this story of mine could be considered threatening. It had to be disguised in some way.

Then I thought of a great story by G. K. Chesterton among Father Brown's adventures: "The Sign of the Broken Sword." There I had the solution. I quote Chesterton:

After the first silence the small man [Father Brown]
said to the other [Detective Flambeau]:
"Where does a wise man hide a pebble?"

And the tall man answered in a low voice: "On the beach."

The small man nodded, and after a short silence said:
"Where does a wise man hide a leaf?"

And the other answered: "In the forest." . . .

"But what does he do if there is no forest?"

"Well, well," cried Flambeau irritably, "what does he do?"

"He grows a forest to hide it in," said the priest in an
    obscure voice.
"A fearful sin. . . . And if he wished to hide a dead leaf,
he would make a dead forest."

There was still no reply, and the priest added still more
    mildly and quietly:
"And if a man had to hide a dead body,
he would make a field of dead bodies to hide it in."[6]

That was what General St. Clare had done. He had killed Major
Murray, who knew he was a traitor, and in order to hide his body
he sent his company into a suicidal action against the enemy in
which most of them were killed. The general escaped, but the
remaining troops knew his crime, court-martialed him and hanged

---

[6] G. K. Chesterton, *The Father Brown Omnibus* (New York: Dodd, Mead and
Co., 1951), 194, 200, 206.

him on a tree, tying round his neck his own sword, which he had broken killing his victim.

Chesterton's imagination gave me the idea. Where to hide a pebble? On the beach. Where to hide a leaf? In a forest. Where to hide a story? In a storybook. There it will be safe, will lie low, remain unheeded, be read lightly as one more story without anyone stopping to gauge its content and to be touched by its message. That was the solution. I had only to take a little trouble to organize a forest, to write the book, and this is now more or less accomplished. Now I can rest undisturbed. I hope the story will pass entirely unnoticed. There goes the little leaf lost in the middle of the forest.

In the year 2050 Professor Newstein, the greatest physicist
    of all time,
made public his famous General Theory of Absoluticity,
which won immediate acceptance and universal acclaim
by all scientists in the world as the unified and
    irreplaceable basis
of modern science in its totality.
Commentators were quick to note
how his very name seemed to be a prophecy
that physics would be brought to its ultimate perfection
    in him,
as Newstein was a providential combination
of the names of Newton and Einstein.
His name and his theory became a symbol
of the great advances of the human race
and of the most glorious moment of humankind's
    long history.

An important corollary of his theory was
what came to be called the Law of Levity,
according to which a heavy body left to itself

without any support would directly go up
until someone or something stopped it.
The equations that defined this upward displacement
were deduced with mathematical rigor,
and the displacement itself
could be calculated beforehand with the utmost exactitude.
Learned treatises were written on that important corollary,
and all its aspects were deeply explored and duly
    elucidated.

A few physicists were slightly disturbed
when they performed some experiments about
    that law.
Sometimes it even happened that when a material
    object was let go,
it fell down to the ground instead of going up,
as was postulated by the law.
Such behavior, which seemed to disprove
Professor Newstein's irrefutable theory,
caused, at the beginning, a certain uneasiness in
    scientific circles,
but soon pertinent explanations were offered
from many important research centers, and all doubts
    were dispelled.

It was insinuated that those who had performed the
    negative experiments
had not understood the theory properly
and that whereas our senses are fallible and can
    mislead us,
Professor Newstein's equations
were absolutely exact and certain beyond all doubt.
Others argued, always in defense of the theory,
that many more experiments had to be performed

before any importance could be given to the few
    negative ones,
and they even hinted that the fact that a few flaws
    remained in the theory
was precisely the mark and guarantee of its authenticity,
because matter is only "statistically organized"
and any theory that was "too perfect" would be, by that
    very fact, suspect.
In fact, philosophers of science pointed out
that nature itself is full of mysteries,
and therefore a certain element of paradox,
bordering though not reaching contradiction,
is inherent in the great truths of nature
and was one more sign of the theory's reliability.
Modern physics has become a very complex science,
while the human understanding is and remains finite
and cannot be expected to delve into all truth
and master every detail by itself.
And so it was argued by not a few
that a certain amount of humility and trust was necessary
and that we had to allow ourselves to be led in such an
    important matter,
on which our material welfare depended,
by the keen mind of Professor Newstein,
whose uprightness and probity were beyond questioning,
rather than rely on our limited intellects and fallible senses.
In fact, reports and rumors also circulated
to the effect that, in some experiments at least,
heavy objects left to themselves had actually gone up,
and witnesses were not lacking to testify to it.
Thus it was a short time before the theory obtained
    universal acceptance,
and all initial objections against it were quickly forgotten.

Only one isolated voice was raised against the theory:
that of Professor Cosense, who was deprived of all
    common sense,
and who shyly and humbly suggested that,
since the important corollary the Law of Levity
seemed contrary to the observed facts,
the whole General Theory of Absoluticity should
    be rejected,
or at least should be left in abeyance
until it could be properly demonstrated.
But no one paid heed to his words. On the contrary,
all the scientists of his own country denounced his
    stubborn obstinacy
before the unquestioned authority of Professor Newstein
and the universal accord of all people of science in the
    whole world,
and he was expelled by unanimous vote
from the Royal Academy of Science.
That same year Professor Newstein
was awarded the Nobel Prize for physics.

I have told that story several times before groups of intelligent
people who want to think out their lives and redefine positions
and with whom I talk, listen, and discuss personal themes with
open trust. After telling the story I ask them whether they have
understood it, and all answer at once that of course they have.
Then I innocently invite them to give some concrete example
from their own experience in which they have apparently continued to hold on to some old position of theirs against all the evidence. When I say that, a sudden silence fills the room. Eyes are
lowered, smiles droop, the air stands still, and the room freezes.
No one speaks. Neither do I. I allow myself and all present to feel
the obstinate resistance human nature exerts against any change,

the blunt refusal to abandon—with respect, to be sure, and with delicacy but with firmness and clarity also—a long cherished belief even when we see with overwhelming lucidity that it no longer fits into reality as we know it. I then repeat in my mind T. S. Kuhn's exact quotation, "Man is an animal admirably equipped to uphold doctrines refuted by factual evidence."[7] No one wants to speak, which makes me suspect that no one wants to think. The silence becomes painful, and soon conversation must be resumed. We talk of other themes and tell other tales. The climactic moment has been quickly forgotten, and the sign of the broken sword has lost its meaning. Father Brown was right. The pebble has remained unknown on the beach, the leaf undisturbed in the forest. "I would be silent," said Father Brown to Flambeau, "and I will." So will I.

---

[7] Salvador Pániker, *Ensayos retroprogresivos* (Barcelona: Editorial Kairós), 35.

SON

OF THE

TRIBE

The African youth listened eagerly to the instructions.
It was the most important moment in his life,
the rite that was to make him a man.
He had reached puberty, and, to be now accepted
into the tribe as a full-fledged adult member,
he had to pass the traditional test that would show
he was strong, sensible, responsible, and trustworthy.
If he failed the test he would continue to be a child
   until another season,
in the shame of his failure and the impatience
   of the long wait.
That is why he was listening with rapt attention,
ready to carry out with prompt exactness
the secret orders given by the elders of the tribe.

These were the instructions:
he had to walk alone into the jungle, without bow
   and arrows,
without spear and shield, and wander and roam through it
until he saw and was seen by a lion,
a rhinoceros, a python, and an elephant.
In no case would he defend himself or run away,
and he should take neither food nor drink,
however alluring the fruits of the trees he saw
or transparent the brooks he crossed.
Once he had obtained the four aims
he was to come back immediately and report to the tribe.
That was all.

The young man departed at once
and directed his steps toward the high-grass prairies
where he knew lions waited for their prey
and where it would not be difficult for him
to see the king of the jungle and be seen by him.

Soon he saw him lounging under a tree
in the carefree majesty of his lofty presence.
He held his breath and waited for the lion to deign
    to look at him.
At last the lion lifted his head, swept the horizon
    with his gaze,
and fixed it for an instant on the svelte, erect figure
of the motionless adolescent.
Their eyes met;
the candidate for man and the lord of the jungle
stood face to face in mutual recognition of their
    acknowledged dignity.
The young man made sure the lion had
    looked at him,
in order to be able to assert it before the tribe,
and went back slowly feeling the blessing of the jungle
    upon himself
and knowing that he had already achieved
the most difficult part of his mission.

Deep in the jungle he soon saw a large python wound
    on a tree
and held its gaze in his eyes without winking.
He also knew the haunts of the rhinoceros,
and watched him and knew himself watched
    at a distance,
reading in the tense air the mistrust
and the warning of the arrogant monster.
Now only the easiest part of the job remained:
    the elephant.
There were many around the place, and it would
    not be long
before he would meet a herd or a lonely male and
    make himself seen.

The elephant does not attack unless he is attacked first,
so there was no special danger.
It was enough to find one, and the task would be over.

But he could not find any.
He went through all the likely places, searched
    for footprints,
scanned horizons, waited in waterspots,
but did not succeed in sighting a single elephant.
For the first time he began to feel hungry.
Until that moment he had not counted days or nights,
had not felt hunger or thirst, but as the search
    prolonged itself
and the fear of failure began to rise within him,
he felt weak and faltered.
How long could he keep up the search?
What would he do if he did not find any elephant?
He would prefer to die of hunger and thirst in the solitude
    of the jungle,
and so save his dignity if he could not save his life;
but the orders he had received bade him
to return alive to the village in any case
and report truthfully all that had happened.
He held on until the very last moment,
but he did not succeed in sighting any elephant
and came back sad and crestfallen to tell the tribe
    his misery.

After listening to him, the chief of the tribe spoke:
"You have passed the test.
We knew you could not meet any elephant because we
had beforehand scared them all away from the
    whole region.
The test was not seeing animals, but telling the truth,

and this you have done.
From this moment you are one of us in full dignity
    and right.
You are a son of the tribe."

To tell the truth is not a mere external commandment that forbids
lying in order to safeguard the welfare of society and enhance the
dignity of humankind. It is much more than that. To tell the truth
is to accept reality, to meet the facts, to yield to nature, to fit in
the cosmos. To tell the truth is to be a whole person, to be one of
a piece, to square with oneself. It is the very integrity of being that
is at stake; it is the thought that fits the facts, and the word that
fits the thought, so that, in the one act, reality, perception, and
expression form a solid and unanimous whole that gives firmness
to existence and meaning to life. The worship of truth is no external rite before a pagan deity but intimate experience of transparent conscience, straightforward vision, and verbal courage. In
Sanskrit the words *truth* and *being* have the same root. To tell the
truth is, in the last analysis, to be.

One of the rites in the Eleusinian mysteries
consisted in stopping the candidate's ears with wax
and tying a blindfold over his eyes so that he could neither
    see nor hear
and then placing him alone in a dark chamber
where he had been told he would hear secret voices
and would see elusive flashes,
which he would have to describe afterward to his masters.
The desire to give an answer to the questions and to obtain
    the initiation
prompted some candidates to describe sounds and lights
imagined rather than experienced.
The true answer, patiently expected
by the masters of the initiation ceremony,

was that outside the hollow sounds of an empty room
and the permanent play of lights and shadows in
   a closed eye,
there had been no supernatural communication
   of any kind.
Sincerity was the first requisite for admission.
Pretending is no qualification for life.

Very often in my life I have adjusted my words to what I was expected to say. I have many times imagined feelings, created experiences, forced interpretations, feigned convictions with goodwill and scanty understanding in order to be able to declare before an expectant and exacting society that I agreed, of course, that I, too, had seen it, had heard it, had felt it, that it was evident and obvious and had always been so and would always be, and that I was proud to be one more willing witness in the list of centuries. I have imagined voices and fancied lights. I have signed manifestos and professed certainties. I have seen what I was asked to see. I have heard what I thought I had to hear. And it has taken me a long time to realize that by doing that I was rendering a poor service to myself and to my tribe.

Back, then, again to candid sincerity, I will say what I feel and will declare what I have seen. And I will also say, without fear or blush, what I have not seen. I have reached the conclusion, hard and healthy, that I no longer want to adjust my statements to what others want me to say, or to what I believe they want me to say, and that from now on I want to say clearly and simply what I truly feel and see and hear and live, and I am ready to say it with all the humility I can muster and all the courage I shall need. That is the true initiation into the mystery of being, the wise ritual of the aborigine that makes an adolescent into an adult.

I have not seen the elephant. Now I can truly be a son of the tribe.

WHERE
ARE YOU GOING,
DEAR LITTLE BIRD?

At a few miles' distance from my own city in India, Ahmedabad, there is a lake, called Nalsarovar (Lake of Reeds), that is an almost limitless extension of shallow waters and is home to millions of reeds, which comb its surface and embellish its face as royal crowns of green majesty. When winter turns to snow in remote latitudes, innumerable flocks of birds of all kinds, who know and prize Indian hospitality, come to seek refuge in its kindly curves, gentle climate, and generous welcome and, year after year, take full advantage of it as honored visitors in a land where every guest is sacred.

As soon as the calendar begins to lean toward its latter months we see them cross the skies in the direction they know with infallible instinct. Who knows their names? Large birds with their slow flight, small little birds of fast moving wings, limited groups of well-knit families, and unending flocks that cover the whole arc of the sky from horizon to horizon over our heads lifted in wonder. And in every case, the ordered flight, the evident hierarchy, the geometric line, the capital V appears as itinerant character over routes marked in blue. To decipher the mystery of the flying V, I quote from the studies of R. Schieferstein and T. Schwenk in *Das sensible Chaos.*

The birds, when they fly in triangular array,
are, so to say, bound to one another by the air that
    upholds them,
or, more exactly, by the elasticity of that air.
Such a group of birds makes up a whole,
and the air that supports them forms part of that whole.
The flock travels in the midst of a "frame of air"
created by the winds and the currents,
which in turn react on each bird in the group.
A comparison will help us to understand this better.
We can often observe in a pond how a swan
    swimming on it

leaves behind a triangular wake of small waves
on which its small chicks are literally carried.
Every moving ship leaves behind it a similar wake.
The natives of Côte d'Or make use of such wakes
for their own transportation.
They manipulate their little boats
until they place them behind the steamer with the
   same speed,
and then they place the boat skillfully
on the front slope of the crest of any of the waves.
The wave then carries them forward with the
   steamer's speed
while they allow their oars to rest.
This is, roughly, the image of the birds in their
   triangular flight.
Each one of them floats on a "wave"
that has been carved in the air by the head bird.
The movements of their wings follow the ups and downs
   of the wave,
and mark the invisible and vibrant "aerial frame"
that envelops and transports those birds.
Thus, each bird flies in an exact and personal spot
of the aerial wake that embraces and unites all the
   members of the group.
Each bird has to spend very little energy,
as the movement of the aerial wave
lifts and lowers its wings in flight, so to say.
If any of these birds possesses any excess strength,
then he does more than letting himself be carried,
he reinforces the wave with his own wing strokes,
thus contributing extra energy to the collective frame
for the benefit of the weaker ones.
These latter can obtain energy from the "air field"
   in motion.

It goes without saying that the bird at the head
also draws energy from that common source.

The flight of the whole flock in formation makes
　　up a whole,
an organism in which the separate birds act as
　　so many organs.
It is a new body, created from the air,
and in which—much as it happens in the sound body
created by an orchestra—each particular instrument
unites itself to the superior unit for the total effect.
The birds, as individual elements in the flock,
are united to one another by the air,
which envelops them as though by elastic threads.
It is the unity and cooperation of the group and the air
that makes the long journeys of migratory birds possible.
The air supports them.
The bird is an aerial being,
and the air will never let it down.[8]

It must have been on one of those days of nature watching, while
contemplating from the vantage point of my friendly terrace the
geometrical flight of hundreds of birds against the open sky, that
the following simple story, or rather vital query, occurred to me.

A flock of birds in V formation
was crossing the sky when a cloud,
which shared the same sky with them,
felt the itch of curiosity and wanted to find out
where they were going
and what plans they had once they reached there.

---

[8] R. Schieferstein and T. Schwenk, *Das sensible Chaos* (Madrid: Editorial Rudolf
Steiner, 1988), 115.

She waited until their paths crossed, and then gently,
without interfering or in any way hindering the flight,
which she knew to be tiresome and important,
she carefully approached the last bird
in one of the branches of the V and asked him sweetly:
"Tell me, dear little bird,
if it can be known and you can say it,
where are you going in your drawn-out and
    purposeful flight,
and what are you going to do there?"
The bird, without for a moment missing a stroke
    of his wings
in rhythmical unison with his companions, answered:
"Oh, if only I knew it!
But I have no idea where we are going.
I only follow my companion who flies in front of me.
I go where he goes and fly in the direction in which
    he flies.
Ask him. He'll tell you."

The cloud went a little ahead
until she was abreast of the next bird;
she asked the same question and got the same answer:
"Ask the bird before me."
She went from one bird to another,
and from the right branch of the V to the left one,
without being able to satisfy her curiosity.
They all told her they knew nothing
and that she should ask the others, as they would
    doubtless know.
But no one knew anything.
Each one followed the one in front of him
without asking questions, and so no one knew
    any answers.

The cloud's curiosity increased all the more
with the repeated failure of her efforts to satisfy it
until she could contain herself no longer
and approached the head bird at the vertex of the V,
even at the risk of disturbing him and distracting him
from his important task as leader of the group.
She apologized accordingly and then asked
where he was taking himself and all those followers
    after him.
Where was he going after all?
The leading bird answered:
"I wish I knew it! I have no notion about it.
All these birds keep pushing me from behind,
and there is nothing else I can do but keep on flying
without knowing where they are taking me.
They are the ones to know it. Ask them!"

Maybe this dialog sprouted in my imagination under the artistic influence of the flying birds in the limpid sky; or maybe perhaps it was the thought of the scientific and poetic explanation of the winged V trail and its help in the effort of the long migration that set me fantasizing about naive birds and inquisitive clouds. But I knew that while doing that I was only projecting onto birds and skies the questions and inquiries of my own experience. Is that not precisely what fables and parables are for?

Around the time I thought of this story I received the visit of a zealous priest who told me his own situation. About thirty years before he had founded a religious institute, which had flourished quietly but efficiently for a good many years. There was fervor, there were needs, there were tasks, and there was enthusiasm, and years went by and numbers increased and much good was done and a good group was formed. But things were different now. There was no longer a clear task or an urgent mission. New patterns of life had emerged in a few years under fast changing

winds, and the founder who had pointed clear directions in the
first years no longer saw himself which way to go. He had been
overtaken by the rapid changes all around and could not see his
way. He declared with total honesty that he no longer saw any usefulness or justification for the group. But what should he do with
them? How could he abandon them? There were several hundred
excellent men and women who had given him the best years of
their lives, and who now, if he failed them, had literally nowhere
to go. He could not leave them in the lurch. He could not tell
them that circumstances had changed and that the ideals and the
tasks that had been valid a few years before were no longer valid
and had to be dropped. He could not bring himself to break the
truth to them, and so he kept going because he did not know how
to stop. He went on, year after year, inventing tasks and hiding dis-
appointments, pushing ahead somehow with the group for lack of
courage to dismantle it. He had tried a couple of times to tell them
indirectly that he was feeling the weight of the years and should
begin to think of his retirement, but his followers had been scared
and had entreated and pleaded with him to remain in the job as
director, since they needed him and wanted his leadership so long
as he could work, which he certainly could do as his health was
strong and his mind alert. Their pleading had prevented his get-
away. So the group went ahead. Who directed whom? Who was
pushing whom? Ask the cloud if you want to know.

How many organizations, institutions, associations, projects go
on simply because they were started one day and no one has
stopped them. There had been a good beginning, a genuine need,
a fervent desire, a concrete ideal, and with that the birth of the
group, the shared enthusiasm, the common front, the concerted
action. Little by little the ideals became blurred and the work
became doubtful, but by then the internal structures of the group
had hardened, vested interests had appeared and grown, the
group needed to ensure continuity, and the members wanted
security, so the norms became rigid, legislation replaced charisma,

and old traditions were invoked to continue doing what always had been done even if no one saw its usefulness any more. They all went ahead because they had to, though no one knew now where they were going. Courageous birds of permanent flight, where are you going? They all avoid the question because none of them knows the answer. And they keep on flying.

I know I am projecting my own question onto others, and I do it willingly and hopefully to obtain companionship in the search and light in the end. It is no longer a question of groups and associations, but of my own life. Where am I going? I have been flying for quite some time, I have crossed oceans and overflown continents, I have covered long distances and advanced along fixed directions, and I keep flapping my wings, I keep working, I keep thinking, I keep talking as I have always talked and listening to the wings and the voices of my companions as I have always done. I am aware that the V formation has helped me, that the "aerial wave" has supported me, that the blue wake has carried me in its trail, and I find comfort in thinking that there will always be some who have watched our flight and have enjoyed a glimpse of beauty and kinship with all of us who fly and dream and live. I could go on in life like this until the end, without asking any uncomfortable questions and without threatening the stability of the group, which goes on flying uninterruptedly; but my curiosity has stirred within me, and I do not want to stifle it. Where am I going? Where is that feathery wave going across winds and currents, true arrow of hope over expectant horizons? Where is my life going?

I know there are answers. If we ask leaders in society, in politics, in thought, in religion, they know well how to give an account of their position and describe ways and identify goals. I know it well. I myself have given answers, have spoken, have written, have encouraged, and have convinced many who asked about the target and doubted on their way. But through my repeating of permanent certainties I have come to feel that they may not be so

certain, and I ask myself whether I am not simply repeating statements I learned and recite by heart. Official answers are not
answers. Those in front keep proclaiming their firm conviction
with efficient emphasis. But my mischievous imagination fancies
that if a cloud approaches them and asks them gently, very softly,
far from anyone's hearing, whether they can tell her where they
are going, they will answer her with a knowing smile to seal the
mutual conspiracy: "Don't tell anyone, but we don't know. All
those behind keep pushing us, and that is all. But, please, let no
one come to know we have told you this. You will be discreet,
won't you?" And the cloud knows how to be discreet. She knows
how to dissolve herself and vanish into thin air, leaving no trace of
herself and taking her secret with her. That is why there are so
many clouds in the sky, and birds love to speak with them.

The cloud, when she heard the leading bird's answer,
felt annoyed and wanted to protest.
It seemed absurd to her that the birds could fly without
     knowing where
and that they would deceive themselves and
     one another
by each one thinking that all the others knew,
while in fact none of them knew a thing.
She thought of exposing the hoax and having done
     with the farce.
She was about to say: "Down with all of you!
Land immediately and face reality!
What is the sense of continuing to fly
when none of you knows where you are going?
This is the end of it!"
But she checked herself in time and remembered that
     she was a cloud,
and as such she had to behave.
For a moment she had let herself be carried away

by the way of thinking of the human beings she knew
    down on earth
and by their way of judging and acting,
which she knew through having observed them
    many times,
and so she had demanded an aim, a target, a direction,
an itinerary in order to justify a flight,
as human beings always did on earth.
But now she became cloud again,
whiff of weightlessness over land and sea,
which did and undid herself in the heavenly game of white
    over blue.
She became discreet again, and, beyond discreet, wise.
She kept quiet after she heard the confession
the leading bird at the vertex of the V had made,
and before the other birds could ask her what their leader
    had told her,
she vanished mischievously with a touch of instant magic.

But before she disappeared entirely,
she whispered in the ear of each one of the flying birds
a parting message with all the tenderness of her soft
    melting heart.
And this was the message:
"Keep flying, my dear little bird, keep flying, and enjoy your
    flight!"

Keep on living, my dear little soul, keep on living! And enjoy your life!

GODS, BIRDS,
AND
HUMAN BEINGS

Pali literature is the repository of most of the early Buddhist scriptures, and in it we find an ancient story whose theme is the same as that of the flying birds and the questioning cloud, and so I sum it up here to defend modern daring with age-old respectability.

The sage Agnana (whose name means ignorance)
had spent all his life meditating
and doing penance in the Himalayas
to obtain the answer to the fundamental question,
which tortured his soul, about the final destiny of all beings
   on earth:
Our world, ruled by the inflexible Law of cause and effect,
and our being, bound by the inexorable Karma
(which are two ways of saying the same thing),
where are they going?
Toward which sublime goal are they ascending,
or into which unfathomable abyss are they rushing
   headlong?

Seeing that he had not much life left on earth,
that he had not made much progress
in the search for the all-important answer,
and that without it his life would remain without meaning
and he would have to be reincarnated again to continue
   the quest,
he decided to address himself to the supernatural beings
whose station is higher than humankind's,
and who, if duly pleased and impressed by him,
could give him in an instant the desired answer,
as they contemplated the whole universe
from the vantage point of their exalted being.

He made his way to the kingdom of the Asuras,
who are closest to human beings,

though superior to them in knowledge and power.
There he addressed himself to a character
who looked knowledgeable and amiable
and placed his query before him:
"Our world, ruled by the inflexible Law of cause
    and effect,
and our being, bound by the inexorable Karma,
where are they going?
Toward which sublime goal are they ascending,
or into which unfathomable abyss are they rushing
    headlong?"
The worthy said he did not know,
but the man could try other people around there,
and someone would surely be able to answer him.
Agnana tried other Asuras without success
until he finally saw that only their chief
could give him any light, and to him he went with
    his question.
The chief answered:
"It is true that I am the ruler of all this kingdom,
and that I know more than all human beings put together,
but I do not know the answer to your question.
Go to the domain of the Devas,
who are gods higher and wiser than we,
and they will have an answer for you."

Agnana's rich merits, accumulated through so many years
of prayer and penance, allowed him to climb one
    more heaven
and reach the kingdom of the Devas.
There again he tried his luck with several inhabitants
until he reached the supreme Deva
who told him very kindly in answer to his question:
"Venerable Agnana, you have posed a very strange question.

It is true that I am wise, much wiser indeed than any
   human being
or even any Deva can be,
but I must confess that I have no answer
   to your question.
No, Agnana, I cannot tell you toward which sublime goal
or into which unfathomable abyss our world,
ruled by the inflexible Law of cause and effect,
and our being, bound by the inexorable Karma,
are destined to go. I am totally ignorant about it, Agnana.
I can only give you a piece of advice:
go to the heaven of the Brahmas.
They are the highest beings available,
and any of them will be able to give you the answer
   you seek
and thus bring peace to your soul and contentment
   to your heart.

Agnana took his last hope with him to the third heaven,
approached respectfully one of the Brahmas,
and stated his question, which by then he knew well
   by heart.
He received a quick answer:
"Do not waste your time.
Only the supreme Brahma can answer you,
and he will do it if you win his favor.
Go straight to him and do your best."
Agnana had to wait to receive an audience.
He observed carefully the behavior of those who
   approached the throne,
made deep bows as he drew near, and proposed his
   question very humbly,
adding that no one in the three kingdoms had been
   able to answer it,

and that was why he had been constrained to appeal
to the only deity that could satisfy him.
The Great Brahma was flattered, smiled widely and said:
"I will satisfy your desire, mortal man and wise ascetic,
as you have shown such an interest in your quest
and it is so easy for me to fulfill your wish.
But before I do I must attend to some urgent business
in another part of my kingdom, so please excuse me.
My servants will meanwhile bring you food and drink,
which you well deserve.
I am coming back at once and will be with you shortly."
Agnana had overcome any desire to eat or drink
but was burning with the desire of knowledge,
especially now that he knew himself to be so close
to the answer at last, and so he said:
"Lord, with you will I go and with you will I come back
and at your side will I remain wherever you go,
and any moment that you find a small break in your
    divine activity
you may turn to me and communicate to me
the answer to my humble question."

The Great Brahma answered, "Come with me
    as you desire."
He took him alone with himself to a corner
of his domains, where no one could hear what they
    were saying,
and lowered his voice to speak in his ear:
"Oh sage, you have gotten me in a fix.
Listen attentively, Agnana, and I will tell you the truth:
this world, which I govern but which is ruled
by the inflexible Law of cause and effect,
and these beings, which adore me as though I could
    change their fate

but which are helplessly bound by their inexorable
  Karma—
yes, I know them, but I have no idea where they are going.
I do not know toward which sublime goal they
  are ascending
or into which unfathomable abyss they are rushing
  headlong.
I just do not know, Agnana, I do not know.
But how can I confess my ignorance before the
  other Brahmas?
They obey me because they believe I possess
  the knowledge
of the secrets of which they are ignorant.
I cannot reveal my ignorance,
because a god's power consists precisely
in seeming to want that which he cannot avoid
and appearing to know that which, in fact, escapes him.
Do you understand?"

And the Great Brahma, smiling benevolently,
took leave of Agnana.

No wonder the birds do not know where they are going. The gods
themselves do not know it. Why should human beings be so keen
to know it?

OF THIS
TREE YE SHALL
NOT EAT

The master wanted to test his favorite disciple
    and told him:
"Take charge personally of the daily cleaning of my
    personal library.
Dust properly each bookcase, each shelf, and each
    book on it,
because dust is the enemy of books,
and books are the repository of wisdom.
You may also page through and even read
any books you want from the whole library
and increase your knowledge in that way.
I enjoin a single restriction upon you,
and you must observe it faithfully
if you want to keep your job and my esteem,
and that is that you must never touch this bookcase
    in the middle.
Do not dust it even on the outside, do not open it,
and never in any way look at the books in it.
This is an important order, and I expect you to obey
    it in all fidelity.

The disciple was glad at the trust the master had
    placed in him,
took to heart the work in the library, dusted it with the
    utmost care,
and then spent all the free time he could get
in reading the marvelous books he was discovering
    day by day.
He understood that this was his best training
and saw in this a deliberate gesture of his beloved and
    venerated master
who thus wanted to train him in the best possible way.
The library was better looked after and better used
    than ever.

After a few days the master,
making sure that he was alone and unobserved,
went to examine the library.
He admired the order and the cleanliness:
not a book out of place and not a speck of dust
    on any book.
He smiled his satisfaction to himself,
as he loved books and loved his disciple.
Then, almost stealthily, he reached the center of the hall
and stood for a moment before the forbidden bookcase.
He opened it carefully and examined it minutely.
He had purposely left a few hidden threads,
some almost invisible patterns in the dust,
certain angles between the books, which would
    immediately give away
the slightest disturbance any interfering hand would
    have caused.
But everything was intact—the dust and the threads
    and the books.
The disciple had kept his promise.
He had not touched a single book in the whole bookcase.

The days passed. The disciple continued cleaning
    the library,
and the master kept secretly observing him.
But the disciple never so much as came near the
    forbidden bookcase.
The master then announced that he would have to be
    away for a month,
as he wanted to go on a pilgrimage
he had planned and cherished for a long time,
and he left his favorite disciple in charge of the library
with a renewed injunction to take special care of it during
    the long absence.

So it was done. The master departed
and came back only after a full month had elapsed.
When he returned, he took the first opportunity to be alone
and searched the forbidden bookcase in the middle
    of the library.
There he verified once more
that not even the long opportunity of a full month
and the safety guaranteed by the master's absence
had shaken the disciple's pledge,
and his stout obedience had kept him away from the
    forbidden books
even in the midst of all temptations.
The master saw it all and reflected in silence.

The next day the master convened a general meeting
    of all his disciples,
placed the favorite disciple in front of all,
and addressed himself to him while all the others listened
    in silence.
He thundered from the start with unmistakable and
    ill-repressed anger:
"You stupid idiot!
You have thoroughly disappointed and wounded me!
You have ruined all my plans!
And to think that I had trusted you and relied on you
    for my work!
I was sure that curiosity would get the best of you
and that you would open the forbidden bookcase and
    read its books,
and I had thought out a plan, which in the long run
would have been for your own good
and the good of the whole institution and its future.
Once I had caught you at fault with the library,
I would have scolded you publicly,

so that, by knowing yourself to be vulnerable
and by learning humility and patience in a public
   reprimand,
you would have acquired the human touch
and the gentle compassion that you still need to round
   out your character,
to add kindness to your steadfastness as a future leader
   of others,
and so to be appointed as my successor
in this institution, which is what I was planning to do
   all the time.
And now you, with your uprightness and self-righteousness
and lack of human curiosity and earthly frailty,
have turned out to be an impossible, intransigent,
obdurate, intractable, inhuman character
and have spoiled everything for me and for my school
   and for yourself.
I had such beautiful plans, and you have ruined them all!
Idiot! There was absolutely nothing special
in those forbidden books, and that is what you should
have discovered by yourself for your own education.
But you never felt even the slightest itch to touch them!
From today you can leave my library alone.
Never mind if it is buried in dust.
What is the use of books when people fail?
You have not been worthy of my trust.
You have failed me. You have wrecked my whole life
and the future of my school.
Depart from my sight!
I don't want to see you any more!"

Query: What would have happened if Adam and Eve had not
eaten the apple?

FIVE
MOUNTAINEERS

A group of five mountaineering friends were climbing
a high and steep peak after a long preparation.
The five were roped together as is prudent for such a climb,
so that if any of them slipped and lost his footing,
the others could unite their strength and lift him to safety
as they had repeatedly and efficiently practiced.
All of their equipment was needed for the sharp climb,
as the summit was precipitous
and any fall to the valley below, quite distant at that height
and forbidding in its primitive and savage beauty,
would of necessity be the kiss of death.
They advanced step by careful step toward the white
    stone vertex
with the fond anticipation of the final conquest.

Everything went well until one of them
slipped badly and dropped heavily toward the
    merciless void.
In his sudden fall he pulled down his next companion,
who could do nothing to steady the first or himself
but, on the contrary, dragged along the next one,
and all the others in turn, until all the five friends,
tied together as they were by the unyielding rope,
fell at once toward the valley to meet a sure death.
The rocks showed no mercy, and,
after the long parallel fall,
the five friends perished in their adventure.

Up in heaven St. Peter got ready to welcome them,
and, as he had watched their risky feat
with keen interest, decided he would ask all of them
a single question, the same for each, and upon the answer
to that single question he would base his decision
whether to admit each of them to heaven.

The first man, who was tied at the head of the rope
as leader of the group, was the first to appear at the
    gates of heaven.
St. Peter, who was ready for him,
asked him kindly and searchingly:
"I have seen that you fell from a great height
onto a wild stone valley, and the fall took a long time,
since you were about to reach the summit when you
    slipped and fell.
Tell me, then, and tell me with all sincerity,
as your eternal destiny will depend upon your answer
    to my question:
What were you thinking about while you fell through
    the air
from the summit to the valley where you met your death?
What thoughts crossed your mind all that while?
Tell me, and I will tell you then where you are to go."

The first mountaineer answered:
"As soon as I lost my grip on the rock
I knew that was the end, and all I thought was
what a fool I was to have got entangled in this
    mad adventure,
which I knew could not end well.
But I had allowed myself to be talked into it,
and now I had to pay the price.
I felt very annoyed and angry,
and in that anger I met my end."
St. Peter told him:
"I am sorry, my son, but you cannot enter here."

The second answered:
"I saw myself fall, and though I understood from the first
    that the situation was desperate, I did not lose all hope,

and, as I was falling,
I tried desperately to get hold of any projection in the rock
with hands or feet or rope, to see whether I could hook
    on to it
and save my life and that of my companions.
I did not succeed, as you can see, and here I am."
St. Peter seemed to think for a moment and then gave
    his sentence:
"You cannot enter either."

The third answered:
"I did not think of myself but of my wife and children.
I felt great sorrow to think that my death
would make a widow of my wife
and leave my children fatherless.
It was with that grief on my soul that I met my death."
St. Peter looked at him with tender understanding,
shook his head and said gently:
"That is lovely, my son, but you cannot enter."

The fourth answered:
"From the very first moment of the fall
my only thought was of God.
I entrusted my soul to him
and asked pardon for all my sins with sincere repentance,
and, though there was not much sense
in pledging to lead a new life
and promising not to sin again when I knew
I would not have another chance to,
I expressed my sorrow for having offended God
and gave myself up to his mercy."
St. Peter scratched his head in thought
for some time, and finally said:
"You did well there, my son, but it was a bit too late.
You cannot enter now."

The fifth answered:
"I saw from the first that I had only a few moments to live.
I opened my eyes and saw all around me
the most wonderful sight the human mind could
    ever imagine.
While we were climbing the summit
I was too engrossed in the task
and exhausted by the effort
and had no eyes for the beauty of the landscape;
but once I was free from all worries
in that magnificent fall through the quickening air,
I could devote myself entirely to enjoy with all my
    grateful soul
the unique spectacle of the mountains and the snow
and the valley and the clouds,
all from the privileged vantage point
of a bird in flight as I felt I was for those few blessed
    moments.
I was in the midst of those happy feelings
when the end came suddenly. That is all."
St. Peter put his hand on his shoulder and told him:
"Go in, my son. This kingdom is for you."
The two of them entered heaven together,
and the gate was closed.

A parable has a point of contact with reality, a lesson, a moral to imprint on the mind when it is told by word of mouth in the open air before a large audience that is eager to take in an image, a phrase, a slogan that lightens the mind and warms the heart. All the rest in the parable is only background music, a frame, verbal greenery to enhance the unique impact of the pointed message. The details are to be forgotten once the main idea has been grasped in all its simplicity and clarity.

In this case the fundamental idea is the importance of living in the present moment with all its possibilities without getting lost in past memories or future worries. All the rest of the parable is only the trappings necessary to complete the picture and bring out the point. And the point here is clear and important. There is always something in the present moment that gives our lives value and meaning, if we can grasp it. And, if we cultivate the precious art of appreciating at each moment the landscape of people or events or nature that appears before our eyes, we shall have gathered a valuable collection of pictures that will give value and prestige to the personal museum of our life. To value each instant is the way to redeem time. To live day by day is the way to rescue the calendar. The idea is as simple as it is practical and beneficent. If we do not know how to live here and now, we shall never know how to live there and then. If we do not enjoy the present, we cannot dream of the future. If we do not have a good time in this life, we cannot expect to have a good time in the next one. As easy as that.

The curious thing is that when proposing this story to all different types of listeners, I have always received unfavorable reactions. In spite of the fact that the context, the approach, the emphasis, and my own way of telling the story underline the single lesson of learning how to live in the present, almost all the listeners take it differently and attack the innocent story tooth and nail. All the mountaineers find defenders except the last one. A few samples of comments people have made after listening to this story follow.

The one who thought of God and prayed is always the one who gets more people to side with him. Have we not been taught that an act of contrition at the last moment wipes away all sins? And if the one who thought of God deserves heaven, no less so the one who thought of his wife and children with almost posthumous love. Also the one who strove until the last moment to try to arrest the fall is defended by many as deserving of heaven, because after all that was his duty at that moment, and he who dies while fulfilling his duty dies well. Even the first simpleton who cursed his luck deserves indulgence, as he recognized his mistake and lamented it in his own way. On the other hand, the last mountaineer garners the worst comments and remarks. They all find him selfish, frivolous, irresponsible, and condemn his levity in looking at birds and clouds instead of preparing his soul for a holy death. They always get my story wrong.

And I always wonder myself and express my wonder before them, as I do here now, at the stubborn and irrational resistance we all put up to the simple task of facing the present. We avoid it by all possible means. We will do anything except look straight ahead. We take refuge in the past with its memories, its nostalgia, or its remorse, or we fly into the future and its dreams, its worries, its fantasies, or its longings. With all our strength we avoid placing ourselves before the present reality, concentrating on what we are doing, and profiting by each moment as it comes in the fleeting existence of the transient opportunity. We are record breakers in the art of escaping, champions of the flight. And that is how I fare with my humble little story! Poor mountaineer and poor parable! They always come out in bad shape after the encounter.

While closing the gates of heaven
St. Peter whispered thoughtfully to himself:
"How can I allow to come into heaven
those who have not been able to enjoy themselves
    on earth?
When will those people down there understand this?"

I bet that you, my reader, are also against my parable. Aren't you?

BLACK
AND
WHITE

A missionary was preaching the Gospel
to aboriginal tribes in the heart of Africa,
and in order to make his catechism lessons
less abstract and more attractive
to the imagination of his listeners,
he had brought from his native land in Europe
a set of large pictures that illustrated, in gaudy colors,
the main themes of his systematic preaching.
That day the lesson was on hell,
and he had brought for the purpose a particularly
    effective picture
in which the artist had depicted the torments of the
    damned in hell
with Dantesque realism and apocalyptic imagery.

The missionary began his sermon with
    great fervent zeal,
and at the right time he unfolded the picture
and raised the tone of his voice
and the darkness of his commentaries
to enhance the effect of the preaching
with the voice and the image.
But he was entirely put out when he saw that
    his listeners
on seeing the picture began to point at some things on it,
make remarks, and laugh heartily.
He lost entirely his train of thought,
had to stop in the middle of the sermon,
and turning to his chief catechist who was seated
    in the front row
and had laughed wholeheartedly with all the others,
asked him with anger and annoyance:
"Can we know why you all are laughing at such
    a serious matter?"

The catechist answered good humoredly:
"But haven't you noticed, Father?
All the people in hell are white!"

This story is not just a good antiracist joke but is a suggestion of something much deeper. Aboriginals in the five continents do not share the white race's concept of sin. The concept of sin as a personal offense to God, the consequent guilt feeling, and the necessary punishment in eternal hell are exclusively "white." It is not a question of discussing, arguing, or convincing anyone, or of being convinced but of having the humble realism and the courageous curiosity to know that how other peoples think can always help us to soften our own ideas, improve our behavior, and enrich our lives. The pictures of the European catechism do not hold in Africa.

AN HONORABLE
RETIREMENT

A true story from the annals of the Indian railways:

A worker in the locomotive yard in the Benares
   railway station
by the name of Ramsharan Chaudhari retired
after working for thirty years at the same job in the
   same place.
His co-workers together with his chiefs organized
   a function
to bid him farewell and pay homage
to his devoted and efficient work for so many years.
He was presented with a gold watch
by the chairman of the railway board,
there were speeches and felicitations, and at the end
the chairman who presided over the function asked
   the worker:
"Would you care to describe for us the work you have
   been doing
so faithfully for these thirty years?"
The good man showed them the long heavy hammer
that had been his faithful companion and his only tool
   for thirty years
and that he had brought with him to the function and said:
"When any train entered or left the station
I had to strike squarely each wheel in each carriage
with this hammer and shout, 'OK!' That was all."
"And," insisted the chairman,
"may we know what you did that for?"
"I never asked, sir," answered the honest worker,
"that is for you people to know."

The good man had been testing the wheels in each train without
knowing what he was doing, that is, without testing them. The
noise made by the wheel when struck by the hammer, which is

different in each case, should tell the well-trained worker whether the wheel is in the proper condition or not; but this man had not been taught that part of the job, and he had never asked. For thirty years he had struck wheel after wheel, shouted OK!, and gone home satisfied with a well-done duty and a well-deserved salary. Never mind how many train accidents happened during those years because a defective wheel was not detected in time. For thirty years he had done what he had been told to do on the first day. Ask no questions and create no problems. Do faithfully what you have been told. If it sounds absurd and meaningless, just think that there are people at the top who know. They are not paying you a salary for nothing. Surely there is something in your task even if you do not see it. The job might have been monotonous and repetitive, but the job satisfaction was full for the man because he knew he was doing his duty. A whole lifetime wielding a hammer, and a gold watch at the end of it. A proud retirement.

Do not ask questions. People at the top know. Even if you see no meaning in what you are doing, keep doing it. All that is expected of you is fidelity and perseverance. Keep hitting the wheels. Day after day. Train after train. Do as you were told on the first day, even if many years have passed since then. Eternal principles never change. Spend your whole life like that, and at the end you will be presented with a gold watch. There will be a party in your honor. And if you are asked what it is you have been doing all your life, you may tell the truth without fear. All of them have been doing the same.

THE
THIEF
AND THE
GOLD

This story is number 36 in the eighth chapter ("Shuo Fu") of Lie Tzu (Liezi), that is, the last paragraph in all his works as they have come down to us. I remember with brotherly pride that the classical treasures of Chinese literature were brought to Europe for the first time by seventeenth-century Jesuits. Among those volumes were the works of Lie Tzu, whose name the Jesuits softened down in the Latin manner to "Licius," and in whose doctrine they admired a contagious charm and an attractive depth that would little by little find their way into the then-remote Western thought. I deem it an honor to tell the story my brothers revealed to distant cultures in a prophetically ecumenical gesture destined to bear fruit in history.

In olden times there lived a man in the city of Qi
whose only ambition was to possess gold.
One day he got up at dawn, dressed,
put on his cap, and went to the market.
When he arrived before a stand where gold was sold,
he took it all and ran away.
A constable saw him and arrested him.
He asked him:
"Why did you think you could take the gold
in front of so many people?"
"When I took the gold I did not see people,
I saw only gold," was his answer.[9]

I am blind. I see only what my passions make me see. I see gold instead of jewelry, clients instead of persons, bodies instead of beauty. I do not see what I should be seeing, I do not see the square and the market and the people and the police who stand watch over the shops. I see nothing. I do not see landscapes and trees and birds and flowers. I do not see nature; I do not see the

---

[9] Lie Zi, *El libro de la perfecta vacuidad* (Barcelona: Editorial Kairós, 1987), 175.

sky; I do not see the clouds crossing through it. I do not see faces, looks, smiles. I see only pleasure and ambition and madness and pride. I see only the yellow shine of the wicked metal. And I lunge to grab it, forgetful of all around me. And my freedom is the price I pay for it.

I am blind. I do not notice things; I do not realize; I do not make contact. I pass through life without knowing where I am passing through; I walk without seeing the way; I live without meeting life. When I walk through the streets I see no one; when I hear words I miss their meaning; when I eat I swallow without taste—always in a hurry, always in passing, always dazed, always running to do something, only to realize after doing it that it was not worth doing, and then always dashing off to something else with the same blindness and with the same frustration at the end. Wild rush of bewildered insanity.

I have lost the sense of proportion in life, the horizon, the per-spective, the distance. The sense of totality, the majesty of life, the eternity of time. In the midst of the large marketplace, the heap of gold is but a faint glimmer, lost among a thousand goods and shops and vendors and people. If I had the calm to see it all and take it all in with an equitable mind, the gold would not command my attention and make me lose my head. Balance in life comes from the capacity to look totally, impartially, universally. To see everything, to feel everything, to ponder everything. Then every-thing finds its place, the horizon becomes clear, and life recovers its meaning. To know how to look is to know how to live.

Through this balance comes the beautiful paradox that gives life to life. Once I free my eyes, I can see the gold as it truly is, and enjoy its splendor without burning with lust for it. The serene look discovers features, reveals angles, weighs carats. It can see in depth because it sees calmly. When the jewelry was watched by a greedy look, it became only a dead object to be grabbed and thrust into one's pocket. The aesthetic pleasure can be felt only when the soul is free. If we want to enjoy things, we must purify the senses. Possession kills enjoyment. I can enjoy sunsets because they are not mine. Inner detachment is the seedbed of art. Beauty reveals itself to the pure of heart. Life belongs to those who do not covet it. If we want to walk with joy through the market of life, we must recover the harmonious balance of the innocent look, the pure regard of mystic contemplation. Now I can look at the gold.

THE
SUPERIOR
HORSE

The following story is number 16 in Lie Tzu's (Liezi's) last collection.

Duke Mu of Qin told his servant Bo Yue:
"You are now old; is there not any among your children
    and grandchildren
who could be put in charge of the selection of horses?"
Bo Yue answered him: "A good horse can be known
by its aspect, its muscles, and bones.
But the superior horse hides itself,
and there is no way to find it out.
When it gallops, it is swift as an arrow;
it stirs no dust and leaves no footprints.
My sons do not have exceptional talent.
They can be taught to distinguish a good horse,
but they are unable to learn how to discover
    a superior horse.
Your servant has a friend called Jiu Fang Gao.
With him he has cut firewood and carried provisions.
In the matter of horses his talent is in no way inferior
to that of your servant.
I ask you to grant him a hearing."

Duke Mu granted Jiu Fang Gao an audience
and entrusted to him the mission to find a superior
    horse for him.
After three months Jiu Fang Gao returned and informed
    the duke:
"I have found the horse; it was in Sha Qiu."
The duke asked him: "What kind is it?"
"It is a black mare," said Jiu Fang Gao.
The duke sent for her, but it turned out to be
    a brown stallion.
Duke Mu, annoyed, called Bo Yue and told him:

"What a hopeless blunder!
Your expert in horses cannot even distinguish
the color or the sex of the animal.
How will he discover a superior horse?"

Bo Yue heaved a deep sigh and told the Duke:
"How far has he reached indeed!
This is proof that his talent infinitely surpasses mine.
Gao observes directly the nature of all beings:
he grasps their essence and drops the accessories,
gets to the bottom and disregards appearances.
He only sees what he ought to see
and does not see what he ought not to see.
He observes what he should observe
and ignores what he should not observe.
This is Gao's method of evaluating things, and it is far
    more important
than the simple art of finding good horses."
The horse arrived and, indeed, it was a superior horse.

This story explores the art of discovering essences, of delving deep, of getting to the bottom. Color and sex do not matter. Words and appearances and publicity do not matter. We let ourselves be carried away by outward impressions, by public opinion, by whims, by fashion, by show, and we judge that the best-looking horse is also the fastest one. We swim on the surface, specialize in the obvious, are experts in the commonplace. That is not the way to live life. That is not the way to win a race.

We are invaded by the culture of superficiality. Voices that are only noises, images that are flashes, ideas that are publicity. Every thought is borrowed, and most people believe what they read and repeat what they hear. Who today has the time to think? Who dares to be different? Who can overcome prejudices, conditionings, opinion polls, statistics, headlines, advertisements, propaganda? Who can be independent, personal, original, and think on his own and draw his own conclusions and hold his own views? These are difficult feats in a rubber-stamp world.

In another passage Lie Tzu speaks of a man, named Que Yong, who could tell whether someone was a thief by looking the accused straight in the eye and who never was found wrong in hundreds and thousands of cases.

The calm of his own eyes, the piercing look, the unerring experience taught him infallibly what was in each person, and he could judge by sheer instinct what would take a bench of judges a long and involved process to decide. That serene look, that innate wisdom, that vital return to the very center of one's own nature to sense, as by spontaneous instinct, what fits in with things as they are and what jars in the total harmony of life and cosmos is the very making of rational beings at their best as crown of creation.

Whether the concern is judging horses or human beings, the best judge is one who is truly in touch with him- or herself, in vital contact with each feeling and emotion, attuned to life, and at home in nature. One must look to the cosmic evidence of the present moment, one's own organism as prime witness, and the smooth consensus of facts and events as verdict without appeal— every human being as judge of creation.

It will be to our advantage to develop that instinct, to trust our hunches, to sharpen intuition, to focus mind and body and senses, and to let the arrow of discernment fly by itself to its unerring target. Only thus shall we be able to find a great horse worthy of Duke Mu of Qin himself.

THE
LOST AXE

Here is another story (number 34) from the chapter "Shuo Fu" of Lie Tzu (Liezi). I find this story particularly delightful.

A man lost his axe.
He suspected it had been stolen by his neighbor's son.
When he observed him, it seemed to him
that he walked like an axe thief,
that his features were those of an axe thief,
and that all his movements and gestures without exception
were exactly those fitting a regular robber of axes.

After some time the man went to dig in the valley and
found his axe.
The next day, when he saw again his neighbor's son,
not even one of his gestures or movements
seemed to him to be that of an axe thief.

Lie Tzu shows here his subtle sense of humor. I would like to know which is the way of walking fitting an axe thief, which way of talking and gesturing, and in what it differs, for instance, from the way of walking befitting a spade thief. But the wary eye distinguishes these traits, that is, it imagines it distinguishes them and fancies it sees in each detail, each movement, each tone and inflexion the telltale gesture with incontestable evidence. Even the alleged thief's profile seemed to be that of an axe thief. Maybe his nose looked sharper.

The prejudiced project their own prejudices onto the facts or persons in question, and then see everything through their own eyeglass, they dye what they see with their own color, fits things into their mold. Isn't his guilt evident? See how he walks, how he talks, how he moves! Every gesture gives him away, every wink betrays him. A look at him is enough to convict him. Why ask for more proof? His very way of acting is more eloquent than all witnesses' depositions and police investigations. It must be he, therefore it is he. See how he behaves. He is walking proof of his own guilt. The weight of the hidden suspicion, nursed in the dark and believed without appeal, is greater than the open sentence of a hundred courts of justice. Mistrust kills relationship.

Husband and wife. Is he, she faithful to me? Is he, she unfaithful? Once the doubt has been conceived, everything is seen from that angle, and every incident adds conviction to a jealousy devoid of proof. If the wife believes her husband deceives her (or the other way about, as there is no monopoly in these matters), she will start to interpret each one of her husband's actions as a new verification of his unfaithfulness. If the husband behaves with some coolness, shows less affection, forgets dates or attentions he never missed before, the wife will decree at one: "There it is! Didn't I say it? He is now interested in another woman, and he naturally forgets me. He cannot hide it, poor man! Don't I know him through and through?" And if, on the contrary, the husband shows himself more affectionate than he used to be, the wife will immediately jump to the evident conclusion, telling herself, if not her neighbors and friends: "Didn't I say it? There you have the obvious guilt. The poor man cannot even dissemble or cover things up. He is entangled with another woman, and so that I may not notice it he feigns greater affection and loads me with gifts and treats and outings. His guilt is showing. Haven't I known him for so long!"

Damned if I do and damned if I don't. It is perfectly possible that the husband was less demonstrative those days simply because he had a stomachache or his business had taken a bad turn or his horoscope was unfriendly; as indeed it is perfectly possible that he was more affectionate on other days because he was truly feeling affection and wanted to show it as he felt it inside. But nothing will help. The lot has been cast. The verdict has been given. The prejudice has won the day. It is evident that he has stolen the axe. Don't you see how he walks?

Believers also project their feelings into their thoughts, both in doubting crises and in fervent faith. Why should this senseless and unbearable suffering come to me? I have my weaknesses, but I have never harmed anyone, and I have served God as best as I have been able to do. If there is a loving and just God in heaven, why does he do this to me? Perhaps God is not what I have been told he is, or perhaps there is no God at all. And if that is the case, would it not be more honest on my part to suspend judgment and declare myself agnostic? And then, at the other extreme, facing the same suffering but at a moment when the mind is firm, faith asserts itself, and we trust that God knows what he is doing, that he can bring good out of evil, and that he sends us trials to test us and reward us. As the angel Raphael told Tobit: "As you had pleased God, it was necessary to send you a special trial." Our reaction depends on our state of mind at the moment. Before examining the facts it may be good to examine our feelings.

Another case of projection of feelings: the optimist and the pessimist in today's variegated world. The pessimist sees everything black, a day between two nights, sunshine between storms, a rose between thorns. Everything goes wrong according to the pessimist, and trouble, boredom, and failure are the laws of life. The optimist, on the contrary, considers the pleasant things to be the rule, and the unpleasant the exception. The facts are the same, but the preconceived judgment gives opposite sentences. We judge events, persons, and the whole of creation according to the pattern we carry inside us, and we do not even realize it. These hidden prejudices cause friction, misunderstandings, clashes. We suffer and make others suffer because of the false opinions we have formed of them, of the wrong intentions we have imputed to them, and the innocent attitudes we have interpreted wrongly. It is time we learn to clear the mind; to erase prejudices; not to judge, as we are told, in order not to be judged; to give others the benefit of the doubt; to accept their innocence so long as the contrary is not clearly proved; to look at all with friendly eyes; and, if a doubt should emerge, never to rush to conclusions but to suspend judgment and wait.

At the end the axe appears, and all is well again.

THE
WISE
SEAGULLS

This is an ancient story that keeps on changing feathers until it
becomes contemporary.

Many years ago there lived in India a wise and
    prudent king
who was deeply versed in the contemplation
    of holy things
and in the understanding of the hearts and minds
    of his subjects.
One day he passed by the side of a man
whom he had never met before,
and while passing near him he felt a sudden and paralyzing
    fear of him.
He asked the man who he was, and he answered
that he was one of his majesty's obedient subjects,
an honest dealer in wood, who,
upon hearing that the king was going to pass that way,
had come, eager to obtain a glimpse of him.
The man looked sincere, but the king was not satisfied.
He had felt the sting of fear,
and his instinct never betrayed him.
He took the man aside, won his confidence,
and asked him more in detail about his attitude
and his feelings on seeing the king.
The man said: "One thought did occur to me
when I saw your majesty, and though it was only
    a thought,
and I put it out of my mind at once, I beg your majesty's
    pardon for it.
The thought was this: I am a dealer in wood,
and I have stored now in my warehouse
a large consignment of precious sandalwood
in which I have invested much money
and of which I don't know how to dispose.

When I saw your majesty, the thought suddenly occurred
   to me
that if your majesty were to die, God forbid,
the funeral pyre would have to be made of sandalwood,
as custom and law require,
and that would give me a welcome chance
to dispose at once of my load.
That was just a passing thought,
and as such I lay it open before your majesty."
The king thanked him and let him go in peace.
He now knew why he had felt ill at ease.
His instinct had not failed him.

**This story is the Indian version, complete with the royal crema-
tion on the sandalwood pyre, of a Zen story retold by Raymond M.
Smullyan in *The Tao is Silent*. Here is the Buddhist version.**

A Zen Master was one day absorbed in meditation
in his garden while the cherry blossoms were in full bloom.
Suddenly he sensed a danger.
He wheeled around but saw no one but his boy attendant.
This upset him dreadfully,
for he had never been wrong before about such matters;
in the past whenever he had sensed a danger,
there always was a danger.
He was so troubled by this inexplicable incident
that he retired to his room, not even coming out for food.
Some of his servants were worried about him
and went up to inquire of his health.
He explained what was troubling him and kept saying,
"I don't understand. I've never been wrong before!"
News of the matter spread to the other servants
   and attendants,
and finally the boy attendant who had been in the garden

came up tremblingly to the master and confessed:
"When I saw your lordship so absorbed in the garden,
I could not help thinking that despite our lordship's skill
    with the sword
he probably could not defend himself
if I at this moment suddenly struck him from behind.
It is likely that this secret thought of mine was sensed
    by the lord."
The boy expected to be punished,
but the master was in no mind for doing so,
being thoroughly relieved for having solved the mystery.[10]

With even greater delicateness and artistic touch, as is to be expected from his consummate skill, Lie Tzu (Liezi) sketches the same situation in a masterly picture. It is the verbal equivalent of a Chinese painting where a few strokes define a whole landscape, and the sobriety of means enhances the effectiveness of the masterpiece. Here it is.

A young boy who lived by the seashore liked the seagulls.
Every day in the morning he went to the sea to play
    with them;
and they came to him by the hundreds, without end.
His father said to him,
"I have come to know that the seagulls play with you.
Catch a few for me, will you?"
When the boy went to the seashore the next day,
the gulls danced in the air, but did not come down."

The seagulls know it. They have gotten wind of it at once. Maybe they do not understand the language of human beings, but they

---

[10] Adapted from Raymond M. Smullyan, *The Tao Is Silent* (New York: Harper and Row, 1977), 176–77.

understand the expression of their faces and the tone of their voices. Maybe they did not hear the father talk to his son, but they saw the son's face the next day and sensed the threat in the look of his eyes. And so they danced their dance in the air, but did not approach. The father wanted to catch them, and that was no game anymore but danger of death. And once the word of danger has been pronounced by human lips, the seagulls sense it with the tips of their feathers on their wings, and they keep clear of the suddenly treacherous beach. The boy has lost his playmates.

And now it is my turn, or rather the turn of a sensible and reliable religious sister of a renowned congregation who confided to me personally the story I now tell.

A nun was in Rome for some days,
and one Sunday morning she went to visit St. Peter's.
While she was walking through the huge square
she felt a desire to talk to someone
in order to discuss, as a tourist and a religious,
the mutual experiences of the holy visit.
She then approached a man who, like her,
was walking leisurely through the square,
and began to talk with him.
Hardly had they exchanged a few general phrases,
when an overpowering sense of fear took hold of the sister,
and she felt in her whole being a burning sense that
   told her,
"This man is very, very dangerous.
Call the police immediately and hand him over to them."
She put some distance between him and her.
Then she looked around but saw no police,
and what could she have done even if she had seen any?
Blind impulses do not convict.
She went back to her lodgings and put the incident
   out of her mind.

The next Wednesday, in St. Peter's square
during his weekly public audience,
Pope John Paul II was dangerously wounded by two
　　pistol shots.
The news shook the world.
The frustrated murderer was captured,
and all newspapers carried his photograph.
When this sister saw it, she recognized the face at once.
That was the man in whose presence three days before
she had felt the dark foreboding.
If the white seagull had been warned about it,
he could have flown to safety.

All nature is one, and it sends its vibrations to whoever can make them out. They are waves on the lake of time, reaching from shore to shore. Whatever is done leaves its imprint; whatever is said wakes an echo; and whatever is thought or felt or schemed in the mind finds its way, too, through secret passages in shadowy tremors and anticipates and announces and informs and warns those who are ready and prepared to be warned. There is a universal sense of familiarity with all that is good, an instinctive experience of feeling at home before a person of God, an inward recognition of goodness when we meet it, a restful trust in the presence of friends. And there is also, in dark contrast, the ominous premonition of the onslaught of evil, the note that jars in the symphony, the event that does not fit in, the rebellious character, the veiled threat of death. The universe speaks. The stars whisper. The breeze informs those who are ready to be informed, nurses friendships, and prevents dangers. There is in us a universal feeling of unity with the whole of creation, which comes to us through our bodies, born of the earth and in close communion with all elements and beings who know the news of the cosmos and want to tell it. It is for us to sharpen our senses, open our minds, broaden our perception. The whole creation is ready to send its message when people listen to it and to one another with the intimate sense that unites all in a common destiny. If we learn to trust our insights, we shall draw closer to nature in heaven and earth and to all creatures with whom we share our earthly habitation and heavenly goal.

And the wise seagulls will continue their winged games in the blue safety of the cloudless sky.

THE
KING'S
SWORD

A merchant was crossing the river in a boat,
when the heavy bag he carried with all his goods in it
fell into the waters.
He reacted quickly, took out his knife,
marked a cross on the side of the boat
over the exact spot where the bag had fallen,
and then waited quietly
until the boat reached the shore.
He then dived exactly under the cross he had marked,
but for all his efforts could not find his bag.

Llui Bu-Wei (Lü Buwei)

Flash of lightning of the present moment. Redeeming instant and fleeting salvation. Here and now. This or nothing. Either you dive now, or you lose your treasure forever. Everything passes, everything flows, everything flies. An instant for the river waters to flow, and the contact is lost; a stroke of the boatman's oar, and the booty sinks into the deep. Life is to be lived moment by moment. Opportunities pass. The instant is just gone and never returns. The boat continues on its course, and the goods are lost.

Here is another version of the same story.

A king who was traveling down a broad river in his
    royal barge
bent over the side to look at the fishes in the waters,
and at that moment his royal crown
slipped from his head and fell into the river.
The king immediately took out his sword and with its point
drew a cross on the waters to mark the spot.
The next day, while transacting the daily business
with the chief minister, the king ordered him to send
    some servants
to fetch back the crown from the place in which
    it had fallen,

which had been duly marked by the point of the
royal sword.

When we are reminded of Heracleitus's saying that we never step
into the same river twice, we at once reflect that it is true because
the river has changed. Its waters now are not the same as those
were at this spot a moment ago, and so the river is not the same.
That is true, but, by immediately thinking so, we miss the deeper
and more practical meaning of the adage: it is we who have
changed. Our life also flows, faster still than the waters in the river.
And so it is that we can never step into the same river twice. It is
not only that the waters are not the same but that the foot that
enters them is not the same and that the mind that rules the foot is
not the same and that the heart that rules the mind is not the same.
Life is change, and each moment makes sense only in the fleeting
instant in which it exists—the cold contact of the naked foot with
the wriggling current, unrepeatable meeting of fluvial pleasure. To
know how to enjoy change is to know how to live.

Not even the king's sword can mark the dancing waters of the
river of life.

THE
HONORABLE
GENTLEMAN YE

In a city of old China lived the honorable gentleman Ye,
who was so fond of dragons that he had drawings
and pictures and sculptures of dragons all over his house.
The dragon is a benevolent being,
a symbol of power and a good omen,
that brings good luck to those who venerate it
as devoutly and fondly as the honorable gentleman Ye.
The supreme dragon in heaven came to know
    of the veneration
in which the honorable gentleman Ye held him
and of the many images Ye had kept of the dragon
and decided to reward such faithful devotion
by going in person to visit the man.
The dragon came down, then, from the heavens,
landed on earth, found the house of the honorable Ye,
and put his head through the door
and his tail through one of the windows,
as he could not get in fully as he was.
When the honorable gentleman Ye saw him,
he was utterly frightened, jumped out of one
    of the windows
and flew for his life, maddened at the sight he had seen.
What he venerated was not the dragon
but the image of the dragon he had fashioned for himself.

Shen Tzu (Shenzi)

**What would happen if God peeped through the window of your
house some day?**

ON PAINTING
DRAGONS

There was a court painter in China
who was once asked by the prince royal:
"What is most difficult to paint?"
The artist answered: "Dogs, cats, horses,
    and similar models."
"And what is easiest to paint?" insisted the prince.
The painter answered at once:
"Ghosts, monsters, and dragons."
On seeing astonishment depicted on the face of the prince,
the artist explained: "We all see dogs, cats, and
    horses daily,
and therefore any defect in their reproduction
    shows up immediately.
That is why they are difficult themes for a picture.
On the other hand, no one has ever seen ghosts, monsters,
    or dragons,
and they have no definite shape. So it is very easy
    to paint them."

Han Fei Tzu (Hanfeizi)

We speak of God with great ease. No one has seen him. We can attribute to him the features that seem to us more fitting for him, and it will not be easy to contradict us. We can paint freely. No one has seen the model. And this very thought should fill us with respect and prudence and reverence when we fashion our own internal images of the divinity. Let us not abuse the freedom to paint what no one has seen.

I often hear religious-minded people say things that make me shudder for the sheer effrontery of their presumption, such as: "God wants you to do this"; "God has punished you for doing that"; "God is displeased with you"; "God is angry with you"; "God will be very pleased if you behave in this way now." To say such things, quite often, is only painting dragons, your own features with a high title. When you tell me that God will be very

pleased with me if I do this, I suspect that what you really mean—
even if you yourself do not explicitly know it—is that *you* would
be very pleased if I did it and to give weight to your assertion and
a selfless look to your request you bring in God and attribute your
wish to him. That stroke of the brush was entirely your own. You
were painting your own dragon for your own convenience. Our
art galleries are full of such paintings. Painters of divine models
have forgotten the consideration and moderation and reserve that
befit a court painter.

These same painters of divine models suddenly forget their
artistic facility and hide their brushes and keep quiet and appeal
in their silence to the mystery of divine things and the finitude of
the human intellect when they are asked to explain the reality of
pain and suffering and the agony that life on earth is for many.
Then they drop their brushes, and their canvasses remain blank.
They have no explanation to offer, no pictures to draw. The models are only too familiar to us for them to attempt a description.
We all know suffering in our lives, we see its face daily and feel its
presence next to us. Then the masters keep quiet. They do not
want to paint dogs and horses. We could tell them that their paintings do not resemble their models, that what they say does not fit
the reality, that their theories are of no use to us. And they keep
quiet. They prefer to go on painting dragons.

The easiest thing to do is to talk of what we do not know. That
is why we do it so often.

THE
VULNERABLE
DRAGON

The dragons in China have the power to transform
  themselves
into any animal they may wish, and so come closer
  to human beings
or avoid them as the case may be.
Once it happened that a Great Dragon,
who was very fond of the company of human beings,
transformed himself into a white dove
so he could be near them and play with them.
He had a very happy time for a start,
fluttering around in their squares, alighting on their roofs,
nesting on the towers of their pagodas,
and eating what kind people lovingly offered him—
a dragon's dream in a dove's dress.

Everything went well until one day when the dragon
  turned dove
innocently approached a gang of mischievous and
  aggressive children
who began to throw stones at him with deadly aim.
The poor dove could not believe his eyes;
he was sure that there must be a misunderstanding
  somewhere
that would soon be cleared up,
but by the time he realized that the children
  meant business,
and dangerous business at that, and decided to take flight,
gain height, and make his escape,
a stone hit him in one of his wings and broke it.
A blushing of blood appeared over his white feathers,
and when the dragon saw it, he knew he was in
  serious trouble.
He was fully aware that until the blood could be stanched

and the wound healed he could not return to his
    original form as a dragon,
for in order to transform his body had to be free
    of any defect.
A wound on the dove's wing
would mean a defect in one of the dragon's legs,
and this could never be, because a dragon must be
a perfect specimen at all times.
He knew this and was afraid.

He tried to fly but could not take off the ground.
He ran fast on his legs with the help of the wing that still
    was whole,
with the hope to increase his distance from the boys
and hide somewhere in safety, but the stones were faster
    than his flight.
Several hit him, and the savage cries of his persecutors
when they saw him lose strength made him lose all hope.

At that moment a man in the neighborhood,
who had heard the shouts, came out,
drew near, took the scene in at a glance,
understood the situation immediately, felt pity for the dove,
took it carefully in his hands, and ordered the unruly boys
to abandon their prey and disperse.
Once in his house he nursed the dove,
cleaned his wounds, gave him food,
and prepared for him a snug, fluffy corner where
    he could rest.
The dove slept in grateful safety.

The good man looked after the dove day by day,
he caressed it lovingly, spoke to it,

and made sure that it was regaining its strength
and that nothing was left wanting.
Soon the dove's wounds healed,
its wings recovered their strength, and its courage
　　came back.
Now it was the Great Dragon again,
and he knew he could return to his original form whenever
　　he wanted.
But in the meantime he also had grown attached
to the family, to the man who had saved his life,
to his wife and children, who all vied with one another
in showering their affection and care upon the dove.
The Great Dragon had often felt his own power,
had seen human beings fear him,
admire him, venerate him, appease him,
but he had never felt loved, looked after, caressed.
That was a new experience for him,
deeper and richer than any he had had before,
and he was loath to leave it.

But a dragon also has duties, which he should not neglect,
and the Great Dragon, who had been absent
from his heavenly quarters a long time, was well
　　aware of it.
There were petitions to be sorted, needs to be provided for,
invitations to be accepted for feasts and celebrations,
and all that could wait no longer.
The people in the family that had protected him,
when they realized that the dove had recovered entirely,
decided to give him back his freedom, took him
　　into the open,
far from troublesome children, and let him fly.
The dove went higher and higher in ever-wider circles,
looking affectionately toward his benefactors

until he was lost sight of in the sky.
Once back in his quarters,
the Great Dragon recovered his original shape and size
    and strength
and went back to his usual routine.

But every year at about that same time,
the Great Dragon turns himself again into a dove
    to relive gratefully
the days in which he experienced the love of a human
    family.
If you happen to see a white dove with a red feather
    in its right wing,
that is the Great Dragon who has come to you.
If you greet him lovingly, you will experience his blessing.

To be vulnerable is to open oneself to love. It is impossible to love
a huge dragon, covered with scales, with his deadly claws,
armored tail, three rows of teeth, and a mouth that belches fire
and smoke. On the other hand, it is quite easy to love a white
dove, even more if it has been wounded by a human hand.

To be vulnerable is an essential step to becoming fully human.
Those who protect themselves with unbeatable armor isolate
themselves from their fellow human beings. Such a one we may
fear or, at most, respect but never love. Distance and safety and
lack of involvement and absence of feelings may create a remote
refuge for a person but will never win a place for that person in
the hearts of humankind. If someone boasts of being indifferent to
all things, unaffected by praise or insult, able to live alone, in need
of no one, and above all events, he or she may achieve some kind
of sterile peace but never a warm human life worthy of the name.

To be vulnerable is to live at close quarters, to invite trust, to
bury all pride, to forgo safety, to embrace life. To know how to
bleed is to know how to love. To risk is to conquer. The wound

on the wing is the crimson price of personal intimacy, and the treasure is worth the price.

To be vulnerable is to be friendly. Out with all barriers, distances, defenses. The knowledge that I can be wounded unites me to my brothers and sisters in the common need of our human condition. When I acknowledge my frailty, I declare that I need others, and I call them trustingly into my life. It is a gracious frailty that brings company.

To be vulnerable is to invite love. Maybe that is why God came down to earth.

ON KILLING
DRAGONS

Chu Ping-Man went to Chili Yi to learn how
  to kill dragons.
(At times dragons may become harmful
and must be eliminated.)
He studied for three years and spent almost all his fortune
until he mastered the subject.
But there were so few dragons
that Chu could not put his knowledge to use.

Chuang Tzu (Zhuangzi)

With the greatest respect to the tradition that so ordered it, with
sincere and deep appreciation of the principles, intentions, dispo-
sitions, and regulations brought into play with exquisite profes-
sionalism and devoted commitment, with my personal gratitude to
the splendid persons who consecrated their lives and dedicated
their untiring efforts to make reality out of those ideals and teach
them to me, and even with a deeply tender nostalgia for all those
unequaled years of generous youth and joyful obedience with outstanding companions and eventful moments in my memory, I
declare today, in responsibility and freedom, that my long ecclesi-
astical studies consisted, for the greater part, in teaching me how
to kill dragons. And I have not met any anywhere.

THE
FLUTE
SOLO

When prince Shuan's orchestra
in the kingdom of Chi gave a flute concert,
there were as many as three hundred flutists playing
   in unison.
A scholar named Nanguo came to know of that,
approached the prince, and applied for a place in his
   orchestra.
He did not know how to play the flute,
but he won the prince's favor
and got the job with a fine pay attached to it.
Everything went well until the sudden demise
   of prince Shuan.
He was succeeded in the throne by prince Min, who liked
   flute solos.
When the scholar Nanguo heard of that,
he fled the country in a hurry.

Han Fei Tzu (Hanfeizi)

I always feel suspicious when many people say the same thing.
There is always someone who does not know how to play the
flute.

In India we tell an even more radical story.

A king had prepared a solemn sacrifice to obtain
the blessings of the gods and goddesses over his kingdom.
He wanted his people to take an active part
in the ceremony, too, so that they would earn
the corresponding merit together with him.
He asked them, in consequence,
to fill a large tank with milk,
so that the precious gift of mother cow
could then be used generously in the sacrificial rites.
The loyal subjects willingly accepted the royal order
and pledged their contribution.

Thus they obeyed their king
and pleased the gods and goddesses at one time,
so that there could not be a more noble and
    meritorious action.
Still, even in such a holy undertaking human greed
    came into play.
The reasoning was simple:
everyone is going to pour in pure milk, and the tank
    is large,
therefore no one will notice anything
if I quietly pour in water and save my milk.
In fact that was the only trouble with the reasoning,
namely, that it was very simple and could, therefore,
    occur to anyone.
The operation was duly carried out,
and when the king approached the tank to bless
    its contents,
he found it full of water.
From that moment he knew what to think of his people.
That is, he realized that at least they knew how to think.

If prince Shuan in the kingdom of Chi had engaged personally all
the three hundred musicians for the royal orchestra, he might
have found that their first concert was a silent solo. Maybe they all
poured water in the tank, and there was no milk for the sacrifice.
Silence for a concert.

Unisons are always dangerous, and not only in flute concerts.

SHIELDS
AND
SPEARS

In the kingdom of Chu lived a man who sold spears
   and shields.
"My shields are so solid," he boasted,
"that nothing can pierce them.
My spears are so sharp
that there is nothing they cannot penetrate."

"What happens when one of your spears
   strikes one of your shields?" someone asked him.
The man gave no answer.

Han Fei Tzu (Hanfeizi)

This story delights me, and I do not know why. And I do not want
to start analyzing it, because it will lose its charm. Maybe the reason is that I am irritated by people who are too sure of themselves, of their ideas and attitudes. These are people who do not
have ideas, they have certainties, and it is a torture to deal with
them. One has to wait until one of their spears strikes one of their
shields. Then watch the fun.

NEW SHOES

In the kingdom of Cheng a man decided
to buy a new pair of shoes.
He measured his foot but forgot the measure at home
and went to the market without it.
There he went to the shoemaker's.
"Oh, I forgot to bring my measure with me,"
he said, and returned hastily to his house.
When he came back to the market,
the fair was over, and he could not buy new shoes.

"Why didn't you try them on?"
one of his neighbors asked him.
"I trust the measure more," he answered.

Han Fei Tzu (Hanfeizi)

Once I had to accompany my mother, who, in order to obtain a certain document, had to submit a certificate to the effect that she was alive. The certificate had to be an official one, which could only be obtained at a particular window in a particular office. After finding the place and locating the exact window we filled out a form, paid the fee, and obtained the sealed and signed certificate that testified she was alive. With it in hand we went back to the first office, submitted it, and were finally given the document we wanted. That is, my mother could not, by showing herself, smiling and saying "Hello!" prove that she was alive; but when she produced a sheet of paper with official letterhead, rubber stamp, revenue stamp, and garbled signature, which stated she was alive, her application was admitted forthwith. Those people also trusted the foot's measure more than the foot itself.

On another occasion I, myself, had to submit an application with my photograph. I had a photo of mine taken to make sure it was the correct size and handed it over personally, together with my application, at the foreordained window. (A window again!)

The god who was at the other side of the window ordered me: "You have to bring a certificate to show that this is truly your photograph." I took the photo, placed it facing him, held it by the side of my own face, and told him with all the reverence due to his exalted position: "Kindly look carefully and tell me yourself whether I am the person in that photograph or not." The god answered: "That is certainly your face, but to certify it you need the signature of a gazetted officer at the back of the photograph, together with a certificate testifying that it is authentic." I made a deep bow before the god and withdrew.

I had no idea what a gazetted officer was, but a friend of mine had a friend who said he knew one such character and was ready to oblige. My photograph passed from hand to hand and came back together with the flourish of a signature and a properly worded certificate. A gazetted officer, who did not know me from Adam and had never seen my face in his life, had certified, thanks to a friend's friend's intercession, that the face in the photograph was mine. What my face had not achieved, his signature did. The god at the window accepted my application and gave me his blessing. The foot's measurement was again more important than the foot itself.

Not all of this story is fun. Han Fei Tzu's story is much more serious and is meant to make us think after we have laughed. The defendant in this trial is not the government's bureaucracy, but our own selves. We, too, allow ourselves to be led in our lives by measurements, rules, certificates, slogans, traditions, beliefs, customs . . . and we forget our own foot. The best measurement for a well-fitting shoe is my own living solid foot in three dimensions as it is at the present moment when I need new shoes. The foot also changes, grows, and is modified by the years and by the treading on a thousand grounds. I cannot go by an old model. It is not enough to quote my size. I want to try the shoe today and see how it fits me. Old shapes are not enough, however well they have gone with me in the past.

If my foot has grown, my heart and my mind have grown also, and so has my way of looking at things, my capacity to grasp new ideas, my hope, and my faith. When I go to the market today I want to take my whole self with me, with all the living and throbbing reality of my dreams, my ideals, my humility, and my joy and so buy the pair of shoes that goes better with the shape of my feet, the choice of my taste, and the money in my pocket. If I have forgotten the measurements at home, so much the better. That will lead me to sharpen my look and to enliven my options. I do not want to let the fair pass without buying a new pair of shoes; I do not want to be choked by the bureaucracy of the spirit.

DEER
HUNTING

A hunter was particularly skilled
in imitating the voices of all the animals in the forest
and used this skill of his to hunt them.
The animals, when they heard their own call,
thought that others of their kind were there, came
    without fear,
and the hunter brought them down with his arrows.
The method never failed.

One day he went out to hunt deer,
and once he reached the proper spot in the forest
he began to imitate their call.
Before the deer could come, however, a wolf heard
    the call,
and thinking he could find food,
as it is easy for a wolf to kill a deer, he turned up at once.
The man was frightened when he saw the wolf,
but he had presence of mind, and to get rid of the wolf
he started imitating the roar of the tiger.
As soon as the wolf heard it, he was scared,
turned round, and disappeared as fast as his legs would
    take him.
But then, drawn by what seemed to be the voice
    of another tiger,
a tiger showed up, and the hunter was even more
    frightened than before.
To get rid of the tiger he imitated a bear's grunt,
since he knew that even the tiger fears the bear and flies
    from his presence.
The tiger, in fact, left immediately, but then a bear came,
and there were no more tricks available.
The hunter had exhausted his repertoire of animal calls.
He was left alone and defenseless,

and the bear pounced on him, tore him to pieces,
   and ate him up.

Liu Dsung-Yuan (Liu Zongyuan)

Imitations are always dangerous. One can play the tiger for a while, but ultimately the bear arrives and the story ends. The only way for a man to last in his own forest is to be a man, and for a woman to be a woman. The best way to give full value to life is to be oneself. Each one of us has his or her individual and exclusive voice, and that is the one to use for dignity and integrity. No imitation of foreign models or animal calls. They tell us our voice is as personal as our fingerprints, and modern gadgets can identify it with forensic accuracy. And no wonder. The voice expresses the character and portrays the person. Maybe the animals, at least in the parable, can be deceived by our imitations, but among us, human beings, we soon come to know, by the tone of voice, the pitch and the timbre, the hurry or the leisure of the syllables, what mood the speaker is in. We can tell whether it is a tiger or a wolf, or perhaps a faithful dog or a purring cat today. The voice speaks with its sounds even before it does with the sense of its words. It is ambassador extraordinaire of the human mind.

We would do well to nurse our voice as we nurse our own identity, never to mimic anyone but to be truly and faithfully what we are and want to be. Let the deer come whenever they want.

FARMERS
AND
HARES

There was a farmer in the kingdom of Sung.
One day, a hare that was running recklessly
dashed against a tree in his field,
broke its neck, and fell down dead.
Then the farmer put aside his spade,
sat under the tree, and waited for another hare to come.
No more hares came, and the farmer became
the laughingstock of the whole kingdom.

Han Fei Tzu (Hanfeizi)

Sometimes we are the hare in the parable. We run about so thoughtlessly through life that we can break our neck against any tree. And sometimes we are like the farmer, twiddling our thumbs leisurely under a tree and waiting for hares to come and break their necks at our feet. Neither of the two attitudes work. When we run, we must run well, and when we tend the fields, we must not put aside the spade. Neither must we fail to take advantage of the hares that may be willing to break their necks around us. Everything has its time—the crops in the fields when the season comes and the surprise hare when it appears. The unexpected enlivens the daily fare.

The interesting point in this parable is that it comes from a Taoist master. Taoism has been accused of passivity, inactivity, indifference to life. That is why the master here meets the objection and makes a laughingstock out of the farmer who puts aside his spade—and of all those who bury their talents and while away their lives. Equanimity is one thing, and laziness is quite another. The secret of life is not in not working at all, but in working in tune with the rhythms of nature in the open fields and in the human body, in the blood and in the seasons, in the full moon and in the noonday sun. The master here depicts two extremes with quick strokes of the brush and leaves them imprinted on our mind so that we may see how absurd and ridiculous both of them are and that we may find, almost by instinct and without the efforts of willpower or the bidding of authority, the middle way that ensures a bountiful harvest without undue haste. No scatter-brained hares and no indolent farmers. No mad rush and no defeatist despondency. No messianic urge to do everything by ourselves and no dejected giving up, saying that we can do nothing at all. The wisdom of the middle way is the great law of life. And that is the quiet lesson of the subtle humor in this lovely parable.

THE
NAIVE
FAWN

A dweller of Linchiang once captured a fawn and decided
to rear it.
As soon as it entered his house, however,
his dogs looked voraciously at it,
showing their teeth and licking their lips.
The man was angered and chased them away
but was worried about what his dogs might do to his fawn
any day.
From that moment on every day he came before his dogs
holding the fawn in his arms,
thus teaching his dogs to respect and accept it.
Little by little the fawn began to play with the dogs, which,
obeying their master's will, became friendly with him.

The fawn grew up and, forgetting he was a deer,
came to believe that dogs were his best friends.
They romped around together with ever-greater familiarity.

Three years passed by. The fawn, now a grown-up stag,
saw a pack of hounds in the street one day.
He came out immediately to play with them,
but they saw him approach and felt within
a wild and murderous anticipation.
They tore him to pieces and ate him up.
While breathing his last, the young stag kept wondering
why he was dying so prematurely.

Liu Dsung-Yuan (Liu Zongyuan)

A young married couple of my acquaintance own a small cat
whom they love and upon whom they shower every attention.
One year they went for a holiday in the country, and they took
their cat with them so that she, too, could enjoy life in the countryside. But the cat had a very hard time and, like the fawn in the
story, almost paid for her holiday with her life. In the city apart-

ment in which she had grown up, she felt safe and secure, she was the boss, and if any other animal showed up, she could count on her human protectors to impose order and guarantee her safety. The cat had lost her own preservation instinct in the presence of hostile animals; she felt secure and had not learned to fly from danger. But now in the countryside there were other cats that were resentful of the intruder who encroached on their territory. There were also dogs of all types, many mischievous boys, and stones on the paths. These stones could, in the wink of an eye, pass from the ground to a boy's hand and from the boy's hand to the cat's flank. The boys in the village had good aim, and a lazy and cuddling pet cat was an ideal target for their missiles. Her masters soon had to lock the cat up in a room in the house to protect her life. She did not seem to enjoy her vacation.

The lesson to be drawn from the cat and the deer is not the moral pessimism that the whole world is bad and one has to protect oneself and not trust anyone if one wants to come out alive from the test. That is not the point. The point is much more subtle and far-reaching and is a basic principle in Chinese thought. It is simply that everything has to be what it is and not pretend to be something else. The deer is a deer; it is made to graze and jump and romp and delight us with its surprise appearances and its joyful pranks. And it is also made to spring into flight on its agile legs as soon as its alert sense of smell brings to its nostrils the faintest whiff of beasts of prey over the horizon. If it forgets what it is and starts playing distractedly with dogs, tigers, or lions, it will end up between their teeth, wondering, as the youthful stag, at such dire unsuspected reaction—unsuspected by those who do not know themselves. The lion will always be a lion, and antelopes of any kind are their favorite meal. But the antelope also remains an antelope and develops its sense of smell and trains its legs for the race whose prize is life.

Confucius calls his fundamental principle "the correct use of names" and bases on it his whole system to organize society and bring peace and prosperity to the world. The following dialog, taken from *Lun Yu (The Analects)*, XIII, 3, in which "the master" is Confucius, explains it.

Tsi Lu said to the master: "The prince of We
is waiting for the master in order to organize
    his government.
What would the master do first?"
The master said: "Surely the correct use of names."
Tsi Lu said: "Is that the thing to do?
You are surely wrong, master! Why the correct use
    of names?"
The master said: "How dull you are, Lu!
The prince puts aside, so to say, what he does not
    comprehend.
If the names are not correct, the expressions do not fit;
if the expressions do not fit, action does not follow;
if action does not follow, the arts and morals do
    not flourish;
if the arts and morals do not flourish, punishments
    do not help;
if punishments do not help, the people do not know
    where they stand.
That is why the prince cares first of all
to use the correct names in his expressions
and that his expressions be turned into action.
The prince does not tolerate there being anything
undefined in his discourses. That is the main thing."

The background situation in the kingdom of We was that the true king was in exile and was considered an enemy, while the actual ministers were in fact traitors, so that each one was what he was not, and the proper order was subverted. That is why Confucius said, with even greater clarity: "Let the prince be prince, and the minister be minister; let the father be father, and the son son; let the farmer be farmer, and the carpenter be carpenter." It sounds like a useless tautology, but in fact it is a universal rule of good government. Let each of these be truly and fully what he is: the father, a good father; and the son, a good son. Let each one honor the appropriateness of his name. Let each one do his duty, ply his trade, use his talent, contribute his effort. Let each one be worthy of his name and also use every object according to the nature reflected in the name—a chair as a chair and a table as a table—and extend that principle and behavior to society itself and to the whole of creation.

By being what we are, we also pledge ourselves to come to be, and help others to be, all that we can and ought to be. There is to be found the source of growth and progress for the individual and for society. If the prince is not a good prince, part of the duty of a good subject is to remind the prince and help him to be what he should be.

Let the deer be a deer and a cat a cat, with all their beauty and litheness and strength. I suffer when I see domesticated animals. I hope that the burgeoning ecologic conscience may reach them one day and liberate them and return them to their joy.

I also suffer when I see domesticated people.

COUNTING
PEANUTS

This story is found in the chapter "Qiwulun" of Chuang Tzu (Zhuangzi) as well as in the chapter "Huangdi" of Lie Tzu (Liezi), a fact that lends it special interest and weight. Maybe its importance is not apparent at first sight, but it is worth looking into for a while.

In the kingdom of Song there lived a tamer of monkeys.
He was very fond of these animals and kept a large number
    of them.
He could understand their desires, and they, for their part,
    could follow
the indications and wishes of their master.
He, of course, had to put aside a good part of the family
    provisions
for their food, and he did it willingly.
But there came upon the land a time of scarcity,
so that there were no leftovers,
and he was obliged to cut down the monkeys' share.
Fearing that they would rebel against him, he decided
    to use a trick.
He asked them: "Will you be satisfied if I give you
twenty peanuts in the morning and thirty in the evening?"
The monkeys raised a ruckus to signal their refusal.
He took time out to think, and after a while he asked them:
"What, then, if I give you thirty peanuts in the morning
and twenty in the evening?"
The monkeys then sat down
and expressed their satisfaction with the deal.

All religions, each one in its own way, teach the importance of the equanimity of soul before pleasure and pain in order to keep one's peace of mind and not be carried away by instinctive likes or dislikes against the conscience's precepts. It is important to achieve the balance, the calmness, the perspective that ensure a clear vision at the time of acting in the midst of all kinds of pulls that seek to condition our actions. My father St. Ignatius consecrated the word *indifference* in this context and grounded on it the architectural structure of his contemplative activity. I quote here, with a thrill of gratitude, the essential text that has accompanied me through life with the uncompromising light of its beeline reasoning. It is the "Principle and Foundation" of his *Spiritual Exercises.*

> Human beings are created to praise, reverence, and serve God our Lord, and by means of doing this to save their souls.
>
> The other things on the face of the earth are created for the human beings, to help them in the pursuit of the end for which they are created.
>
> From this it follows that we ought to use these things to the extent that they help us toward our end, and free ourselves from them to the extent that they hinder us from it.
>
> To attain this it is necessary to make ourselves indifferent to all created things, in regard to everything which is left to our free will and is not forbidden.
>
> Consequently, on our own part we ought not to seek health rather than sickness, wealth rather than poverty, honor rather than dishonor, a long life rather than a short one, and so on in all other matters.
>
> Rather, we ought to desire and choose only that which is more conducive to the end for which we are created.[11]

The word *indifferent* falls right in the middle of the inspired section, as center of gravity of the doctrine it upholds and the way of

---

[11] Ignatius Loyola, *The Spiritual Exercises of Saint Ignatius,* George E. Ganss, S.J., trans., (Chicago: Loyola University Press, 1992), 32.

life it inspires. The iron logic of the unrelenting argumentation conquers our reason; the perspective of eternity itself reduces objects to size and levels out obstacles; and the noble generosity of its burning faith draws us toward the last consequences of religious fervor enlightened and sustained by divine grace.

This "indifference" in no way means or connotes any kind of passivity, stoicism, or fatalism. It is rather the ardent expectation of the soldier in the battlefront, always ready to receive orders that will determine the time, place, and direction of the offensive; or it is the active vigil of the hunter, finger on the trigger but open to any quarter on the horizon in which the prey may show up; or it is the restrained strength of the horse impatient in its whole body to jump into the race but obedient at the same time to the slightest hint of rein and bit and bridle to mark its forward dash. Controlling emotions does not in any way mean that they are lacking.

Hinduism also has its own word and its own tradition in this fundamental chapter of the science of the spirit. The Sanskrit word is *samabhava*, which can mean "even mind," "parallel feeling," or "horizontal judgment." It is the unbiased balance of the serene mind before pain and joy. Its foundation is the law of karma, according to which all that we now suffer or enjoy is the result of our own actions in previous births, and, consequently, equitable and necessary. *Samabhava* is acquired through the practice of "the couples," that is, the planned endurance of pairs of opposite sensations (such as heat and cold, hunger and satiety, sadness and joy) without ever letting oneself be carried away by the impression of the moment, as the thought of one of the poles helps one to meet the other with calmness of mind. The great virtue that can be observed in the lands of India is that enviable equanimity of soul before prosperity and adversity, which has left its imprint on the Indian character and forms part of its heritage alive today with consoling freshness.

Buddhism on its part delves into the universal experience of human suffering and seeks its cure in the stilling of the desires that break the inner balance of the mind. This was the "Principle and Foundation" of Buddha's first sermon after he obtained illumination:

This, oh monks, is the Noble Truth on Suffering.
Birth is suffering; old age is suffering;
sickness and death are suffering;
union to what is not loved is suffering;
and separation from what is loved is suffering;
as is the nonobtainment of what is desired;
that is to say, the fivefold attachment to the senses
is suffering.

This, oh monks, is the Noble Truth on the Origin
    of Suffering:
what takes us from birth to birth is the will to live together
with the lust and craving that find gratification here
    and there—
the craving for pleasure,
the craving for existence,
the craving for power.

This, oh monks, is the Noble Truth on the Extinction
    of Suffering:
the extinction of that craving through the perfect stilling
    of desire,
the letting go of it, the expelling of it,
the parting with it, the not giving way to it.

This, oh monks, is the Noble Truth on the Path
that leads to the Extinction of Suffering:

it is this Sacred Eightfold Path,
that is, proper belief, proper aims,
proper speech, proper comportment,
proper life-outlook, proper effort,
proper attention, proper contemplation.

To complete the picture, Islam appeals directly to God's supreme will, which is responsible for the world's order with a sovereign freedom and power and which is not for humankind to question or to doubt. Whatever happens to those who surrender without reservation to God is his most holy and adorable will, and in that unshakable and intimate faith is found the inspiration and strength to overcome feelings of attachment or rejection that spring within us as we meet the daily reality of our lives. The eternal creed comes to help day-to-day behavior, and God's will overshadows the whims of humankind.

To this universal platform of philosophies and beliefs comes now Taoism with its leisurely step and its amiable smile, and its contribution is, typically, a story. Taoism does not deal in speculative thought, eloquent rhetoric, long penances, or fervent devotion. It deals in monkeys and peanuts, and, quietly and good-humoredly, without seeking to persuade or forcing an answer, it tells a story, makes us smile, and says no more. It tells us that, after all, twenty and thirty come to the same as thirty and twenty, that all turn out to be fifty in the end, and that it is not worthwhile to make a fuss to obtain a change that is in reality no change at all. It tells us to take things as they are and to eat the peanuts as we get them. If now it is twenty, it will be thirty later, and if we first get thirty, we shall get twenty next time. It even allows us, if we so wish, to make a little fuss about it, as the monkeys do, since after all they do it to amuse themselves. They know perfectly well that everything in the end will come to the same, but they get up with mock fury, put up their show, listen to the man, and show again their satisfaction at having made the man think of saying the same thing in a different way—which is what human solutions always come to. And once the comedy has been successfully staged, they go back to eat their peanuts with perfect relish, whether they are more or less. They do not even bother to count them.

Meanwhile the roving philosopher who has told the tale, has leaned back on the trunk of the tree under whose shade he was sitting, and has fallen asleep in his childlike innocence, feeling totally indifferent (or experiencing *samabhava,* or being empty of all desire) toward what we may do or fail to do about his story. He only wanted to entertain us for a while, and he has done it. We, in all likelihood, shall continue counting peanuts.

THE
TIGER
SKIN

A lamb was afraid of wolves and could not be at peace
until he found some way of protecting himself from
    their threat.
He finally had an idea; he obtained
the skin of a dead tiger and covered himself with it.
Now he felt secure and began to strut around with firm step
and to graze without any worry on the green pastures.

Suddenly one day, while he was grazing in the fields,
he saw a wolf that was approaching him from afar,
and he started to tremble and shake like a leaf.
He had forgotten he had the tiger skin on.

Fa Yen

We wear the tiger skin, but we forget we have it on. It remains on
the outside. It does not change us on the inside, does not affect
our behavior, does not influence our lives. We hold enough beliefs
to give us strength in adversity, clarity in doubts, joy in life; and
yet we go about worried and bewildered and sad. We shake like a
leaf as soon as the wolf shows up. What we need is a tiger's heart
and paws and strength, to feel within us the courage and the
power to roar and to go forward and to master any situation. Just
by putting on the tiger skin we achieve nothing. We must believe
with all our soul.

REPEATED
GOSSIP

Once, when Dseng Shen went to the district of Fei,
a man who bore the same name committed murder.
Someone went to Dseng Shen's mother and told her:
"Dseng Shen has murdered a man."
"Impossible," she answered,
"my son would never do such a thing,"
and went on spinning quietly.

A little later someone else came and remarked:
"Dseng Shen has killed a man."
The old woman went on spinning.
Then a third man turned up and insisted:
"Dseng Shen has committed murder."
This time the mother became frightened.
She threw the spindle away, jumped over the wall,
    and ran away.
In spite of the fact that Dseng Shen was a good man,
and his mother trusted him, when three people accused
    him of murder,
his mother, for all her love for him, could not help
    doubting him.

Yang Siung (Yang Xiong)

What will happen when not three but hundreds of people repeat
the same thing? They can make us doubt anything, and they can
also make us believe anything. We would be wise not to get upset
and jump the wall. Better keep on spinning. The innocent son
will soon come back home and clear up the misunderstanding.
There may be many people by the name of Dseng Shen.

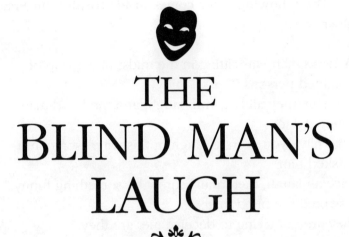

THE
BLIND MAN'S
LAUGH

Chao Nan-Sing (Zhao Nanxing) was an intellectual in the time of decadence of the Ming dynasty. When he was unfairly dismissed and ostracized by influential courtiers, he took refuge in his writings and exposed the abuses of the government by means of fables. The following story comes in his treatise "In Praise of Laughter."

A blind man was sitting in the midst of a group of
   sighted persons.
Suddenly they all began to laugh, and the blind man
   laughed too.
"What have you seen to laugh in this way?" someone
   asked him.
"Since all laugh, there must surely be something funny,"
   answered the blind man.
"They are not trying to deceive me, are they?"

Not only the blind laugh when others laugh. Many more do it, so as not to let it be known that they have not caught the joke. Sometimes even all laugh, and no one knows why. No one has gotten the joke, but someone has started to laugh, and they all follow. One must laugh in order to appear intelligent. One must agree, even if one does not know what one is agreeing to. One must follow the group in order to belong to the group—even when the joke is not funny at all.

That is what the blind man had seen, sightless though he was, and that is why he laughed.

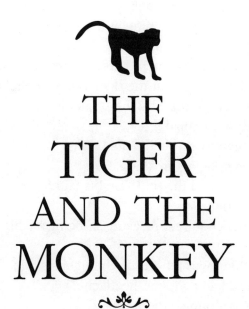

THE
TIGER
AND THE
MONKEY

The titi is a climbing monkey with long sharp nails.
A tiger that felt some itching at the top of his skull
asked a titi to scratch his head.
The titi scratched so much that he bore a little hole
into the tiger's skull, but the tiger was so delighted
with the relief afforded by the scratching
that he did not realize it.
The titi began to eat the tiger's brains
without his noticing anything.
The tiger declared the titi to be his faithful and
    devoted friend
and experienced great pleasure in being by his side.

When nothing was left inside the tiger's skull,
he began to feel a violent headache.
He wanted to punish the traitor,
but by then the titi had found refuge in the top of a tree.
The tiger roared, leaped high, and died.

Tan Kai

Lesson: Do not allow anyone to eat your brains.

The word *coconut* is used colloquially in Spanish to denote the human head. Young people in Spain are very fond of an expression they have repeated so often it has become a kind of motto of the new generation. It is: "Do not let anyone eat your coconut," which obviously means do not let yourself be brainwashed. Monkeys also like coconuts.

THE
CONSIDERATE
THIEF

In the city of Dingchou there was a chicken thief
who every day stole a chicken in the neighborhood.
His friends upbraided him for it
and at length succeeded in convincing him
that what he was doing was wrong.
He resolved to mend his ways and told his friends:
"You are right. What I do is wrong; I will never do it again.
Henceforward, instead of stealing a chicken every day,
I'll steal a chicken every other day."

That is the way with our resolutions. Compromise. Halfway. One step to the right and one step to the left. One finger in every pie. One bow to God and one to the devil. We never say it so plainly, but that is the fact. Don't do it fully and don't leave it fully. Half and half. Of course we are not going to steal a chicken a day. That is too much by any account. We must be moderate and considerate. We must listen to those who wish us well and advise us well. No more daily thefts. But we have to live somehow. It is enough sacrifice to make a chicken last two days. We hope our gesture will be appreciated. We keep our addiction and earn the respect of all at the same time. A fair deal for all. We are surely not expected to change radically. A chicken thief is a chicken thief. And will be so for life. But he knows how to behave and please his conscience and his stomach. He finds the happy solution. And goes on stealing chickens.

What exactly are our chickens?

TEACHING
HOW TO
SWIM

A man was walking by the riverside
when he saw someone who was about to throw
a small child into the water.
The child was shouting in utter fright.
"Why do you want to throw
that child into the river?" asked the passerby.
"His father is a good swimmer," was the answer.

Llui Bu-Wei (Lü Buwei)

The effort to obtain liberation is strictly personal and nontransferable. There are some people, particularly in the East, who would have us believe it is enough to have recourse to a guru and pledge fidelity to him in order to attain salvation. It is enough to submit, to surrender, to obey. The guru knows, the guru acts, the guru has already arrived where we are all meant to arrive, and he will pull after him, as the engine in a train pulls the cars, all those who remain faithful to him. The guru is a great swimmer. You have nothing to worry about.

I do not worry. But if I do not know how to swim and they throw me into the river, I will drown.

The true guru is the one who teaches how to swim.

THE MOP

An instructive experience of Zenkei Shibayama, abbot of the Nazenji Monastery in Kyoto:

The following incident happened to me
during my training days in the Nanzenji Monastery.
Near the monastery was the private house of Roshi Bukai,
who had hired it for some time.
Before going to live in it, my master, Roshi Bukai, asked
    me to clean it.

The previous tenants had left the house in terrible
    condition.
I managed to clean the rooms,
but when I reached the bathroom the difficulty increased.
Besides, it was a day in August, the heat was unbearable,
    and I hesitated.
I felt as though I was being asked to touch something
    horrid and revolting.

I had not noticed it, but my master, Roshi Bukai, stood
    behind me.
He took off his sandals, tucked up his clothes, and,
without saying a word, pushed me aside, took the mop
    from my hand,
and began to clean the lavatory.
For a moment I stood aghast.
But at once I went toward him, took the mop from
    him, and,
forgetting myself, began to scrub the bathroom.
Roshi looked at me for a moment and said calmly:
"You have a mop in your hands, and you are unable to be
    one with it,
being disturbed by the distinction of clean and dirty.

Are you not ashamed of your training?"
I will never forget how ashamed I felt at those words.[12]

The important lesson of this incident is contained in the words of
the master: "Be one with the mop." To identify oneself with whatever one does. To pull down frontiers. To avoid judgment.
Whatever I do or I touch is not to be taken as something foreign
to me, as something outside me, which pleases or displeases me,
looks clean or dirty to me, attracts or repels me. Such divisions
create opposition, and opposition generates suffering. This holds
good for events, persons, things, and, of course, mops, If I consider a mop as something hostile that leads to troublesome work,
I shall create within myself a feeling of repugnance, and my body
and my mind will rise up in protest. On the contrary, I can consider the mop as an extension of myself, of my own hand, which
makes use of it to extend its reach. Do we not say something similar of a writer's pen, a painter's brush, a sculptor's chisel? They
are cherished tools, which fit into the artist's hand and obey the
creative imagination as though they were part of the body. And
the work of art is born. Can we not say the same of the lowly
mop that fits even more snugly into the worker's hand to help
with the work? Every tool is worthy. Every object is an extension
of the human body. Such a consideration brings peace to the
heart and joy to one's work.

The mop does not mind scrubbing floors. If I become "one
with it," I will not mind either. Further still: the mop enjoys scrubbing floors, because that is what it is for; and if I, for the time I
am to work with it, identify myself joyfully with it, I will enjoy it
also. Trouble and protest are over. Why should I be scrubbing
floors while others enjoy themselves dancing? Those grumblings

---

[12] Adapted from Zenkei Shibayama, *Las flores no hablan* (Madrid: Editorial
Eyars, 1989), 182.

will only embitter my work. Let the dancer identify with dancing, and the cleaner with cleaning. The dancer, if he chose to, could also complain that he does not like his partner, or does not feel like dancing at the moment, or that he is tired and would like to go away but cannot. The activity as such does not matter. What matters is the attitude. And the helpful and healthy attitude is one of readiness to do what one has to do with sincere commitment and without misgivings, the facility to identify with the dancing partner or with the cleaning mop.

The point at this moment is not the solution of social problems or the leveling of inequalities and the end of injustice. We will surely work for that and fight and strive to establish a just order in the world. The point here is to live in the best possible way within the circumstances in which we must live, to avoid painful and useless friction, to take life as it comes, to smooth out unpleasant events and balance our reactions. To identify with all we do is the way to obtain peace.

Shibayama draws this conclusion from his own experience. We must be one with the situation, must go beyond all restrictions. We must be happy if we are happy, sad if we are sad, or seated if we are seated; we must be one with our situation at this very instant and in this very place. That is the essence of real discipline. What a sublime lesson to draw from a humble mop.

I cannot help a last mischievous comment. The master finally got his disciple to clean the bathroom and avoided having to do it himself. Lovely rascal!

LET THE
DOVE LIVE!

Zenkei Shibayama has repeated the following parable several times in his writings.

A gentle dove once saw a wild fire
raging all over a large forest,
and wanted to put it out.
Being so small, however, she could not save the situation,
but she could not give up.
Feeling an overwhelming compassion within,
she began to make trips from a faraway lake to the forest,
bringing every time a few drops of water in her beak.
Before long her strength failed her,
and she fell on the ground dead,
without having obtained any tangible results.[13]

I respect the narrative of the author, but I would not have killed the dove. I would have let her fly so long as she could in her mission of mercy toward the forest, the animals, nature itself. And I would have let her rest before becoming exhausted, to recover her strength for the next task. She need not die. We need not die for every cause worth a sacrifice. What is important is that we work, that we fly, that we help even if it is only a few drops of water to put out fires and quench thirsts and bring hope again to those who have lost it. What matters is that we can be doves when there are so many fires.

The main teaching of the parable, which is almost lost sight of in the midst of the sorrow caused by the tragic death of the dove, is that we must keep on doing all that we can do even if we get no "tangible results." We know from the start that we cannot put out the fire, but that is no excuse to shrug our shoulders and let the forest burn. We must bring our drop of water. Why must we if it is of no use? Because it is of much use indeed. Our action lets the

---

[13] Adapted from Shibayama, *Las flores no hablan,* 139, 200.

world know that there is someone who minds if the forest burns; our action speaks when all keep quiet. It rouses opinion and wakens consciences; it gives witness before all those who watch the white path of the dove against the red glow of the forest fire.

Our action has an even more vital use: detaching us from the compulsive need to obtain "tangible results" in order to believe that our work is valid and our life worthwhile. Such an action can teach us a fundamental lesson in life, which is how to work even if we get nothing, how to give witness even if no one pays attention, how to carry water even if we do not put out the fire, the wisdom to do our duty without worrying about results. We cannot extinguish fires; we cannot solve the problems of the world; we cannot "get" anything. But we can live, we can fly, we can have faith and lift our eyes and cherish our hopes. We can be a streak of white against the red despair of forlorn humankind.

That is why I do not want the dove to die. We do not need her tragic end to emphasize the teaching. On the contrary, we need her repeated flights and her inspiring presence. Let her go on living to fly over other fires, to guide other eyes, to teach other hearts. So long as there are doves to cross the skies, be they blue or red or grey, there will be hope on earth.

HOW MUCH
IS LEFT?

A Hindu saint had spent his life doing penance
to reduce the burden of his past wrongdoings
and speed up the cycle of reincarnations
that were still left for him to go through
before obtaining the final liberation.
The successive births the soul has to go through
before the ultimate illumination are thought to be
	very many,
and the holy man calculated there would be only a few
	left for him
and felt curiosity to know the number.
So the saint asked God, in virtue of the merits
he had acquired with his penances,
to be gracious enough to reveal to him
how many reincarnations were still left to him.

God was indeed gracious enough to answer him
	and told him:
"Look at the tree under which you are sitting."
It was a very large and very leafy tree beyond measure,
and the saint contemplated with wonder its green
	luxuriant foliage.
"Well then, there are as many reincarnations left to you
as there are leaves on this tree," said God.
When the holy man heard the answer, he started jumping
	for joy
and shouted in ecstasy: "Why? Only so few!"

At that moment all the leaves of the tree fell to the ground,
not even one remained on the branches,
and in that same instant the holy man attained illumination.

"I consider that the sufferings of this present time are as nothing
compared with the glory to be revealed for us." (Romans 8:18).

THE
PROCRASTINATING
ANIMAL

The story is told that in one of his military campaigns
Alexander the Great met Diogenes,
who was quietly basking in the sun,
half naked, by the side of a river.
Alexander, who had not been tutored
in his youth by Aristotle himself for nothing,
respected and secretly envied wisdom in all
    its manifestations.
He had heard about Diogenes,
the unconventional philosopher who lived in a tub,
contented with the bare necessities of life
and who somewhat superciliously looked down on people
who did not seem to find it so easy to live that way.
Alexander took the opportunity to approach him in person
and converse with him modestly,
becoming again a student for a while,
in the midst of all his military glory.

Still, he could not keep his army waiting, and,
sooner than he would have wished, he had to put
    an end to his visit
and take leave of the philosopher.
The impression that brief conversation made on him
was so great, that the conqueror of worlds
told the philosopher of the tub:
"I am going now, as I am bound to continue
performing feats for history to record.
But from this moment I pray to heavens that,
in the life that awaits me in my next incarnation,
I may not be Alexander but Diogenes."

Diogenes did not let the occasion pass, and
    answered quickly:
"Why wait until your next incarnation?

You can lead my life from this very moment if you
   so desire.
The river is wide, and the sun is not sparing with its rays.
There is plenty of place for another tub here."
And he laid down in the sunshine while Alexander
   mounted his horse.

The belief in the transmigration of souls, common in the East, can prove very useful. There will always be another life. There will always be another chance. There is time for everything. There is time to be Alexander, and there is time to be Diogenes. Let us then be Alexander at our ease, conquering empires and writing history, and then we shall have all the time we want to be Diogenes, or at least we shall have the consolation to think that we shall be Diogenes even if in fact the opportunity never comes. It is very comfortable to believe in a series of reincarnations, because it gives us the solace to think that we are going to do in the next what we leave undone in this one. The trouble is that the chance never comes. Alexander remains Alexander. He does not get to the tub.

Of the many definitions that have been given of human beings to set them apart from all other animals, there is one that is particularly sharp and carping, and it is this: the human being is a procrastinating animal. Humankind delays, postpones, puts off. That is humankind. All the other animals act on the spot, react on the spur of the moment. They live by the hour, they live minute by minute, bringing the totality of their being to the full demands of the present moment. Human beings, on the contrary, stop and think and hesitate and leave constantly for tomorrow what they perfectly could and should have done today. They think that they should give themselves a well-earned and needed rest, but they decide they will do it later and go on working to the detriment of their health and their mood. Or, again, they think they should undertake an important work, but they think again and decide they will do it later, with detriment to the job and to themselves. That is the sorry art of upsetting the order of things—wanting to be Diogenes when one is Alexander, but continuing to be Alexander, wanting to change, to improve, to attain liberation, to take flight . . . but leaving it for the next incarnation. A little prayer to the gods can settle everything. Conscience is stilled, and the military campaign goes on. And the visit to Diogenes—and who has not visited Diogenes at some time in life?—serves no purpose.

In practice many people seem to believe in reincarnation. And not only in the East.

TELL ME VERY GENTLY

This deeply beautiful and tenderly gripping narrative is very popular in Sufi circles. This is the version of Awad Afifi the Tunisian, who died in 1870.

A stream, from its source in far-off mountains,
passing through every kind and description of countryside,
at last reached the sands of the desert.
Just as it had crossed every other barrier,
the stream tried to cross this one,
but it found that as fast as it ran into the sand,
   its waters disappeared.

It was convinced, however,
that its destiny was to cross this desert, and yet there
   was no way.
Now a hidden voice, coming from the desert itself,
   whispered:
"The Wind crosses the desert, and so can the stream."

The stream objected that it was dashing itself against
   the sand,
and only getting absorbed and that the wind could fly,
and this was why it could cross a desert.

"By hurtling in your own accustomed way you cannot
   get across.
You will either disappear or become a quagmire.
You must allow the wind to carry you over, to your
   destination."

But how could this happen?
"By allowing yourself to be absorbed in the wind."

This idea was not acceptable to the stream.
After all, it had never been absorbed before.

It did not want to lose its individuality.
And, once having lost it, how was one to know
that it could ever be regained?

"The wind," said the sand, "performs this function.
It takes up water, carries it over the desert,
and then lets it fall again.
Falling as rain, the water again becomes a river."

"How can I know that this is true?"

"It is so, and if you do not believe it,
you cannot become more than a quagmire,
and even that could take many, many years;
and it certainly is not the same as a stream."

"But can I not remain the same stream that I am today?"

"You cannot in either case remain so," the whisper said.
"Your essential part is carried away and forms a
    stream again.
You are called what you are even today because you
    do not know
which part of you is the essential one."

When he heard this, certain echoes began to arise
in the thoughts of the stream.
Dimly, he remembered a state in which he—
or was it some part of him?—
had been held in the arms of a wind.
He also remembered—or did he?—
that this was the real thing,
not necessarily the obvious thing, to do.

And the stream raised his vapor into the welcoming arms
    of the wind,

which gently and easily bore it upward and along,
letting it fall softly as soon as they reached the roof
   of a mountain,
many, many miles away. And because he had had
   his doubts,
the stream was able to remember and record more strongly
in his mind the details of the experience.
He reflected, "Yes, now I have learned my true identity."

The stream was learning.
But the sands whispered: "We know,
because we see it happen day after day and because
   we, the sands,
extend from the riverside all the way to the mountain."

And that is why it is said that the way in which the
   Stream of Life
is to continue on its journey is written in the Sands.[14]

When they tell us that we must deny ourselves, die to ourselves,
give up all that we have and all that we are, sacrifice the Self as
the ultimate and definitive sacrifice, it is good that they speak to
us gently and lovingly, because we are not prepared for such talk,
and it hurts us. It hurts us to deny ourselves, to leave ourselves, to
diminish, to surrender. It hurts us as it hurts the stream. What will
happen to me if I let go of my very self? What will a stream be
without stream bed, without water, without banks? Who assures
me I will be born again? What awaits me beyond the desert?
Reasons and arguments are not going to convince me. Or they
may convince my head but not my heart and my feelings and my
wavering. But if a friendly voice in a gentle tone recites to me a
poem, proposes a fable, tells a parable, that may help me with the
reassuring touch of a farseeing prophecy.

---

[14] Adapted from Idries Shah, *Tales of the Dervishes* (New York: E. P. Dutton,
1970), 23–24.

The tale of the sands touches me with the pointed charm of its profound simplicity. I know it is true. I know that the sands are right. They are standing witnesses of the transformation of the waters, they have seen them rise and be dissolved in the heights, and they have seen them come down again in joyful rain that builds a living current rushing to become sea. But the stream does not know all that. The stream sees only its waters losing their level and being sucked by the sands. And the stream fears. All that it knows about itself is that its end is near, and its innate preservation instinct makes it resist the apparent destruction. The sands understand its fear, and so they do not argue, they are not in a hurry, they do not get angry. They speak slowly, closely, lovingly to instill trust and soften the test. And the stream finally understands, gets ready, surrenders. Happy the hour when the stream becomes cloud and begins to fly!

I know that in order to cross the desert I have to cease being a stream. Say it to me very, very gently, for I am afraid to fly.

PLASTIC
SURGERY

A very ugly man had already resigned himself
more or less to live with his ugliness,
when he began to hear reports
of the advances made by plastic surgery
and saw the possibility of improving his facial appearance.
By then he had also saved up a considerable sum of money
and could afford a long absence from his job,
so that after completing the necessary formalities,
he went to the United States,
was admitted into a plastic surgery clinic,
and put himself in the hands of expert surgeons
for all the time that would be needed to obtain
   a satisfying result.

The surgeons were fully successful in their task,
and after many and involved operations,
the man could exhibit a model face that looked
   like something
straight out of a classical Greek sculpture workshop.
The transformation filled him with satisfaction,
and he felt eager to go back to his village
and show his now-beautiful face
to all those who had known his ugliness.

There was only one problem, and that was
that the transformation had been so perfect
that no one recognized him,
and so he was deprived of the joy of springing upon them
the surprise of his newly acquired beauty.

**Please, do not change so much that we may not recognize you on
your way back. Leave out some little shortcoming, that we may
make you out.**

NEEDLEWORK

I am writing this book, and by my side my mother,
who is already ninety-six, is doing needlework or,
more exactly, crochet, weaving with white patience
by means of the hooked needle the unending thread
into the sophisticatedly elaborate pattern
that comes out of her hands line by line
with the infallible symmetry of trained craftswomanship.
Her eyes, which do not see much now,
guess the goings and comings of the thread between
    her fingers;
her memory, which now fails her sometimes
in names and dates and faces, prompts to her
    without hesitation
the never written and always remembered sequence
of the quick moves in the textile hieroglyph;
her hands, now painfully carved by heedless arthritis,
direct with steady skill the silver path of the flying needle.
And on her lap gather little by little
the folding waves of clean air framed in white cotton loops.
Work of art in a home workshop of noble ancestry.

I stop my typewriter for a moment and ask her:
"What are you crocheting now, mother?"
She answers without looking up and without stopping
    for a moment
her fast-moving fingers, "A bedspread, my son."
"For whom is it?" I ask.
"For my last granddaughter," she answers.
I know that crocheting a bedspread takes a long time,
but I also know that she has finished others,
and that she calculates, strip by strip, the measures
    she has to cover,
and at the end the work turns out

perfect and even on all sides, whatever its size.
She now thinks of her family while she crochets,
and remembers all one by one,
to reach them all with her motherly affection
woven into the immaculate fabric.
Then she becomes thoughtful and says:
"I don't know whether I'll be able to finish it,
but at least it keeps me busy and helps me pass the time.
I don't know what I'd do if I could not work."
And she goes on crocheting.

I then think to myself. Blessed be the day when my mother learned needlework. She did not guess then she was acquiring faithful company for lonely old age. Now she finds distraction in it for the long days, enjoys the beloved task, sees herself still useful and very much united with the whole family to whom she presents her work. And at the same time she takes it quietly and leisurely, as she does not have to meet a quota or a deadline, and knows very well that if she does not finish it does not even matter, because the memory and the intention of her last work will remain and fill hearts. That is why every stitch bears joy, and the whole bedspread becomes a lesson in life with its dedicated wisdom and its unruffled calm. It is a work of love that lightens the burden of living.

My thoughts go on rambling. The bedspread as such does not matter. Mother, herself, does not keep track of how many she has completed and how many she will complete. It does not even matter whether the work is finished or not. What matters is the work, the distraction, the dedication, the love. Perhaps the last granddaughter will not come to know about the bedspread destined for her. But even then the work will have been valid and beneficent. It will have helped to better spend the monotonous days of a courageous old age. Therein lies its worth.

I go back to my work at the typewriter.
I am writing a book. A book that,
they tell me and I deep down believe,
will be widely read, will do good to its readers,
will last for some years in bookshops and libraries,
and will contribute in some way to guide some,
enlighten others, and encourage all.
The book is, of course, this one, at which I have worked
    with zest
until I have come to consider it of special importance
    within my own work.
I want to finish it and publish it, see it in the hands
    of my friends,
and feel the satisfaction of a finished job.

And now for an instant I look again at my mother and
    then at myself,
at her needle and at my typewriter, at her work and mine,
and a strangely revealing light suddenly shines in my mind.
I thought my work was important,
while my mother's work, in itself, was not.
One bedspread more or less did not matter, while
    one book more,
in particular this book I am about to finish now,
could be considered important in its message and its fruit.
But now I smile to myself under the light of the sudden
    inner liberation
that makes me see how my book is only one
    more bedspread.
What does it matter whether I finish it or not?
What does it matter whether it is published and read or not?
The world will be the same,
and my readers will continue their lives as they always did.
The truth is that I write books as a distraction,

as a way to pass the time, to spend the days.
I do not know how to do needlework, but I know
  how to type,
and that is my game. That is all, and I see it now with
  redeeming clarity.
Why to worry about one book more or one book less?
Why to worry about all my books for that matter?
Let us play at being writers.
That thought frees the mind and puts to flight the
  seriousness of the task,
the responsibility of the undertaking, the urgency
  of the message,
the gravity of the mission—and a good riddance that is!
Let us do needlework.
There are still grandchildren waiting for a bedspread.
That is a good excuse to keep on working,
to act as though we were doing something, and doing it,
by all means, with true commitment but with
  absolute freedom.
We now know that the bedspread may remain unfinished,
and no harm is done.
It is a pleasure to write a book this way.
At leisure. No hurry. No bondage.
It is a pleasure to live this way.
With the hands full, and the heart free.
To work by all means with joy and zest
but without enslaving complexes that make me pretend
to want to redeem the whole world with my labors.
One more bedspread for another granddaughter.
Joy in the family and distraction in old age.
The cheerful faith to love life and use time
and to value the simple work to be done at each age.
And the spontaneous detachment
that can drop the work at any time without any fuss.

The value of our life does not depend
on the number of bedspreads we crochet.

I look at my mother, thinking to tell her all this, but there is no need. She knows it. She does it. She has always done it this way, working without rest on this or that but ready to drop the work when it was not for her to do it anymore. She has taught me this lesson without words, has shown me the way by walking herself. Simplicity of life in hardworking cheer. Industriousness without pretentiousness. Doing what we can, without anxiety for what we cannot. Working and waiting. Walking and breathing. Living life and enjoying it. Is that not the best way to prepare ourselves for the life in the City of God?

The book is over. One more bedspread. The needle can rest for a while.